The Divine Investment

Dennis "Will" Roach II, Esq.

DEDICATION

In honor of my loving mother, Glenda Lowe Roach, who decided long ago to make the Divine Investment, and has consistently chosen to deposit her time in eternity.

CONTENTS

INTRODUCTION

Our time on earth is barely a blip on the radar of eternity, a brief moment on the stage of life followed by an incalculable and unimaginable existence after death. We stride along the sands of time toward the sea of eternity and are totally incapable of turning back.

Against this backdrop of mystery and overwhelming wonder, we are forced to make a practical and daily choice of eternal consequence: Will we wisely invest our lives in eternity, or foolishly spend them on things which will not survive the fire of God's judgment? It is a choice which will define the way we live. It is a choice for which we will be held accountable.

The seed of this book was planted in my heart when I visited a local hospital to comfort a friend whose father was on the verge of death. Little did I know that my friend's father would pass away shortly after my arrival. I was stunned. However, in the shock of those moments God implanted in me a crystal clear understanding of both the brevity of life and the urgent duty to wisely prepare for the epic moment when we see Christ face to face.

The purpose of this book is to encourage and equip you to make what I have coined *The Divine Investment*. We have been blessed with the opportunity to invest our lives in eternity, and we cannot afford to fail to invest our all and our best for His all and His best. Wisdom will not allow us to hedge our bets. We must seize our time and buy into eternity. This is the heart of *The Divine Investment*.

That day in the hospital changed my life forever, and my prayer is that the Holy Spirit will use this book to impress a divine urgency upon your heart as you prepare to hear those glorious words, "Well done, good and faithful servant" (Matthew 25:23).

7

CHAPTER 1
DEFINING THE DIVINE INVESTMENT

August 30, 2011 was a day I will never forget. My understanding of life, time, and eternity was forever altered within that 24 hour span. It began like an average day, with a flurry of activity. The dog needed to be walked, the kids needed to be taken to school, and my wife and I needed to get to work. Like most days, everything fell into place and we were off and running.

Sometime before lunch I decided to make a trip to the local hospital with my business partner to encourage a friend who was at the bedside of his gravely ill father. Upon our arrival, my friend asked us to run back into town to pick up lunch for him, and we gladly agreed. When we returned with his lunch just a few minutes later, my friend greeted us with the news that his father had passed away. I was shocked and overwhelmed.

In what appeared to be a very small space of time, the father of my friend had passed into eternity. I distinctly recall the profound impression I received after hearing of his passing. It was as if time stood still for a moment and God seized the opportunity to impress upon my soul a simple yet profound understanding of the nature of our existence on earth.

LAYING THE FOUNDATION

As time passed, the simple truths I so keenly understood that day in the hospital burned within me, and I began to desire to share them with the body of Christ. They are the foundation of this book, and the driving force behind the idea of *The Divine Investment*. They are summarized as follows:

1. Our time on earth is incredibly short, but our time in eternity is immeasurably long;
2. As Christians, we will stand before Christ in judgment for our works done on earth; and
3. We should intentionally invest our lives in preparation for that moment.

I wish words were capable of expressing the feelings I had in the intensive care unit just after these truths hit me like a cinderblock. I understood that I would soon pass into eternity just as my friend's father, and that my life would be replayed before Christ in judgment. I was reminded that although my salvation had been bought by the blood of Christ, I would have to give an account of my works (Romans 14:12, I Corinthians 3:13-15, Revelation 22:12).

In those brief moments I felt in my soul an intense mixture of holy fear and resolution. Fear arose because I knew I would be standing before a holy God who would righteously judge my works. However, from this fear there also arose a determined resolution to spend the remainder of my days preparing for that moment, so that I could "be confident and unashamed before Him at His coming" (I John 2:28). It was horrifying, and redeeming.

I now consider the lessons of that day to represent a loving warning from my Father. It is our task to live with our eyes wide open to the brevity of life and the magnitude of eternity, to make the most of every opportunity in preparation for our glorious encounter with Christ. It would be foolish to disregard His word and fail to live with urgency. Thus, I propose we make the Divine Investment.

DEFINING OUR TERMS

In order for us to move forward together, we need to define the term "*Divine Investment*." First, let's take a moment and look at the word *divine*, which is defined as something "of, relating to, or proceeding directly from God or a god."

(Def. 1a. Merriam Webster Online, n.d. Web. 17 Sept. 2013). When we call something divine we are typically speaking of something that comes directly from God, or something so good that it metaphorically could have come from God, i.e. chocolate covered strawberries, a baby's smile, etc.

We have *divine aid,* such as an angel sent by God to save the life of an individual. We have *divine inspiration,* by which God spoke through the prophets of old. There is *divine providence,* which is the work and provision of God in the affairs of men. Most importantly, we have *divine love,* which is best illustrated in the blood of Christ poured out on the cross for the salvation of our souls. Divine is an awesome word because it reminds us of our awesome God!

Investment, on the other hand, is defined as "a commitment, as of time or support." (Def. 5. The Free Dictionary Online, n.d Web. 17 Sept. 2013). We commonly regard an investment as something given now in exchange for something which will be of greater value at a later date.

Investing involves a measure of faith that the return will exceed the investment, or, for example, your twenty dollar stock in *company x* will one day be worth much more than the twenty dollar investment. Therefore, a good investment is considered a wise choice, whether it be an investment in relationships, money, or time.

Now, let's tie this together. When I speak of *The Divine Investment,* I am speaking of investing your life and your resources in eternity. The Divine Investment is *divine* because our ability to invest in eternity originated in the mind of God.

In Jeremiah we are told that "before I formed you in the womb I knew you" (Jeremiah 1:5). Paul stated "He chose us in him before the creation of the world" (Ephesians 1:4). Jesus did away with the notion we are the creators of our destiny when he said "You did not choose Me, but I chose you and appointed so that you might go and bear fruit" (John 15:16).

No one can rightfully claim to have imagined themselves into existence, nor can anyone legitimately believe he has the power to hold the cells of his body together. We are here only because God chose to put us here, and we remain only because He affords us air to breathe.

We have been given the divine opportunity to offer our lives to Him only because He has chosen of His own will to desire that we give Him our all. It is only through the plan of God and the sacrifice of the blood of Christ that we are able to make our investment in eternity.

On the other hand, the Divine Investment is an *investment* because it requires a commitment of our lives and resources in hope of receiving a far greater eternal return. It is also an investment because this exchange involves a large measure of faith.

Most would consider it folly to take their time, talents, and resources and use them in the building of an invisible kingdom. Many would argue it is a bit risky and foolish to trade away a life easily pleased by sensual pleasures for the great unknown of the afterlife. After all, common sense teaches us that a bird in the hand is better than two in the bush.

We cannot see the afterlife, nor is there a long list of people who have been there and returned to report verifiable information. We have read about streets of gold and a place without tears, death, or suffering, but we have also read about suicide bombers inheriting harems.

However, to make the Divine Investment is to humbly trust in what God has said about the unseen, and to choose to spend the remainder of our days investing our time, talents, and resources in eternity.

The Divine Investment takes place in those profound moments in time when the will of God perfectly intersects with the submitted will of the believer, and all eternity stands witness to the event.

For example, you make a divine investment when you invest your time in the life of a younger believer in hopes of leading them to become a man or woman of God, when you build a relationship with a lost person, comfort a sick believer, or sponsor a child in a foreign country.

Investing your life will inevitably involve at least two factors: the hand of God in providing the opportunity, and your hand in taking part. God will lead you to an opportunity and give you the tools to complete the ministry. You, in turn, will recognize the opportunity and take the time you could have spent on other things and invest it in the person or task.

Assuming your teaching and ministry were sound, your work will one day bear eternal fruit, and you will stand before Christ unashamed of your work as it passes through the fires of judgment. This is the blueprint of the Divine Investment.

THE NECESSITY OF THE INVESTMENT

As Paul stated, "we are God's handiwork, created in Christ Jesus to do good works, which *God prepared in advance for us to do*" (Ephesians 2:10). The stage has already been set. Our role in this grand drama is simply to play the part God has given us.

He has planned the event. He has organized the cast. He has set the time and place. This is our God-sized and predetermined lot in life. We have been set apart as servants of God. Cherish your role.

If you make it a priority to invest your life in eternity, God will develop within you a heavenly urgency to make the most with what you have been given. By focusing your life on eternity you will afford yourself a greater number of opportunities to obediently invest your time and resources for His glory and the eternal benefit of souls, including your own.

Your life will become a grand preparation for the moment when you stand before Christ in judgment. Along the way, as God gives you the ability to recognize opportunities, you will capture moments in time you would have otherwise failed to seize.

If you follow God's script, your life story will be composed of countless moments in which you invested your time in others, substituted your calendar for his divine appointments, and took opportunities to invest your time and possessions in His purposes.

What an awesome and wonderful story in which we take part! What a great responsibility we bear to be found faithful! Join me as we focus the remainder of this book on the age-old steps we must take to consistently make divine investments in the Kingdom of God.

CHAPTER 2
GO BIG OR GO HOME:
THE CALL TO REPENTANCE

I enjoyed the peculiar pleasure of taking an evidence class in law school under a most interesting professor named James Jeans. Professor Jeans was one of a kind. He was full of wisdom, an infectious sense of wonder, and had an extremely large heart for his students. There are certain moments in time when we realize we are in the presence of greatness, and this was one of those times for me.

Although I was in my early thirties and married with three children, sitting under the tutelage of Professor Jeans made me feel like a little kid in the lap of Santa Claus. I soaked in his wisdom, taking frantic notes and hanging on every word. He was a walking proverb, and he shared them frequently.

Professor Jeans passed away just before I graduated, but his legacy survives in his students. The title of this chapter is one of his oft-quoted maxims: "Go big or go home."

To make the divine investment and go big with our lives, we must first pass through the door of repentance. There is no substitute for this first step. Repentance begins by recognizing we are bent toward putting the thoughts and demands of eternity on the backburner.

Although we are well aware of the brevity of life and the immensity of eternity, and although we know that we will stand before Christ in judgment for our works, we often fail to allow these truths to govern our behavior.

In our crowded and busy lives, we focus on the things of earth much more frequently than the things of God. Rather than living with a sense of urgency and considering each day as possibly our last, we take life for granted. We assume there will be many more days to come.

This mindset leads us to make ourselves as comfortable as possible in the here and now and fosters a neglect of the reality of the eternal. This is a side-stepping, a back-sliding from our responsibility to seek first his kingdom, to hunger and thirst for righteousness, and to make the most of every opportunity (Matthew 5:6, 6:33, and Ephesians 5:16).

When a teenager becomes obsessed with himself, his grades, his relationships, or his sports or hobbies, and fails to see his school as a mission field, he has lost sight of eternity. College students fail to invest when they assume they have been given four free years to dwell untouched by the call to make disciples on their campus, serve in a soup kitchen, visit a prison, or minister in a local youth group.

Parents ignore eternity just as adeptly as their children. The stay-at-home mom may become so absorbed in her children that she fails to maintain her time in God's Word and prayer, her time with other women, or her ministry in her church. She assumes there will be time for those things after the kids are grown, and misses precious opportunities to grow and be a minister Christ in her home *and* community.

A loss of focus on eternity is also evident in fathers who place their careers and their love of work above *everything*, and in fathers who give their hearts to their televisions every night rather than to their wives and children. Sadly, the silent but indisputable reality of eternity is missed, diminished, or lost in these and countless other examples.

I am reminded of the warning of the prophet Amos: "Woe to you who are complacent in Zion" (Amos 6:1). We love to "take life easy; eat, drink and be merry" (Luke 12:19), but our earthly pursuits and creature comforts cannot have priority over our relationship with the Father. It is our honor and our duty to take part as He accomplishes His will through us on a daily basis.

God forbid that we resemble the foolish man, who, after making life quite comfortable for himself, made plans to build bigger barns, not knowing that that very night his life would be demanded of him (Luke 12:16-20).

Our focus must change if we are to walk in the light of eternity. We must begin to see each day as potentially our last, and each opportunity to minister Christ as a priceless chance we cannot miss. We need to repent. Through repentance we stay on course in our journey to see the face of Christ.

We need to ask God to identify areas where lukewarmness has replaced fire, where comfort has triumphed over labor, and set them aside forever. We need to beg God to give us strength to re-embark into the sometimes rushing river of the Kingdom of God, so that when we reach still waters we can be confident they were not created by us in our pursuit for comfort.

John the Baptist prepared the way for Christ by preaching repentance. Christ began his ministry by preaching repentance. Peter preached repentance at Pentecost.

Repentance is the basic act of turning away from sin. It is a submission of all that we are to the person of Christ, and involves a changing of the mind and the heart, regarding how we desire to live. It is an act of ultimate surrender to the lordship and control of Christ. When we repent, we relinquish our right to the control of our time, our bodies, our relationships, and our wills.

Unfortunately, many people think we repent only at the time of salvation. This is an incomplete and dangerous view of scriptural repentance. Repentance is not something we do *only* when we receive Christ: It is something we do throughout the entirety of our lives. It is an ongoing and important practice of the will in the life of the believer. It is a fruit of a heart exposed and humbled before God.

Note how John addressed the church at Ephesus in Revelation 2:5: "Consider how far you have fallen! Repent and do the things you did at first." This was a letter to a group of believers who had persevered and endured hardships for Christ. If the church at Ephesus existed today, we would most likely consider it a church to be imitated, yet they were in dire need of repentance for forsaking their first love.

We are not unlike the church at Ephesus. We must consistently lay our lives down before God on the altar of repentance. A repentant heart confesses and renounces sin, admits that human power is incapable of overcoming sin, recognizes the atonement of the blood of Christ for sin, and seeks the power of God to overcome the sin.

If we are to realign every aspect of our lives to the reality of eternity, we must constantly be about the business of repenting of everything impeding us in this pursuit. We will find ourselves continually returning to a heart broken before God, begging for His mercy, and asking for strength to complete our quest. Viewed in this light, repentance is an incredibly powerful aspect of our preparation to meet Christ.

As we drill deeper into repentance I would like for us to consider the possibility that we need to repent of our lack of what I would call *godly ambition*, or what has historically been referred to as *zeal*.

Somewhere along the way this ancient and insatiable impulse for the things of God appears to have become the exception rather than the norm. We are comfortable with *a little* godly ambition, but are petrified by *relentless* ambition. We are quite impressed when we see zeal in others, but are careful not to let the fire burn out of control in our own lives.

I propose that we need to regain a mindset that is absolutely white-hot with ambition to stand before Christ unashamed, with treasures in heaven before us and a long trail of good works behind us. Since Christ was not merely advising or encouraging us, but commanding us to store up treasures in heaven, I see no reason why we would not seek to place a treasure trove at His feet.

We are in danger of being deceived if we fail to recognize the lie which says that godly ambition is out-of-place within the Christian life. This lie is typically caught rather than taught. In other words, this lie is usually learned or caught by watching and instinctively imitating the behavior of other Christians.

The evil of this lie is that it leads us to believe that it is perfectly acceptable to live a comfort-driven, cozy Christian life without intentionally, proactively, and *ambitiously* living life in light of the weight of eternity. This lie would have us believe it is okay to be passionate about our hobbies and our sports, our entertainment and our comforts, but that it is out of place to be passionate about our King.

Imagine trying to convince the Apostle Paul of this lie as he bowed his neck to Nero's henchman, or to Peter as he demanded to be crucified upside down. Go and tell that to Jim Elliott just before the spear plunged into him, or to Mother Theresa as she reached down to pull the untouchables from the ditches. Would this lie have held weight with Christ when zeal for His Father's house consumed Him in the temple, among the masses, or on the cross?

We have been played as fools by the deceiver of the nations. The enemy has somehow succeeded in stripping away the fire in our bellies and replacing it with a couch on our hindquarters. We can no longer allow our enemy to discourage us from being zealous in our pursuit of God. God have mercy on us, and restore us to right thinking.

Consider the contrast between a person whose lifestyle reflects the lie, and a person whose lifestyle reflects a zeal for the things of God.

The man or woman who lacks ambition for eternity is perfectly at ease attending church, praying occasionally or even daily, reading the Bible, and avoiding moral failures. Urgency is unheard of, comfort carries the day, and the biblical lifestyle evidenced by the believers in Acts is as foreign as our neighboring galaxy.

A life fully set on fire by ambition for eternity looks quite different. Church becomes a place where we worship the one we so anxiously wait to see, and a place where we seek to give of our gifts rather than get. Prayer becomes the very lifeline of our relationship with Christ, and our only hope of attaining the wisdom necessary to see opportunities as they present themselves.

In prayer we desperately beg for God to use us in ways greater than we can imagine. Scripture becomes our food, and avoiding moral failures becomes a deeper pursuit of holiness reaching the very things we allow our eyes to see, our ears to hear, and our hearts to think.

Before we move forward, let's make sure there are no misunderstandings regarding a question or two some may have at this point. First, I am in no way saying that our salvation is based on works, but only by grace through faith in the blood of Jesus Christ. Nor am I advocating a selfish ambition which pridefully seeks to outpace our brothers and sisters in Christ.

However, I am advocating a selfless love of our King and others, illustrated by a passionate desire to please Him and to faithfully execute our duties as a child and steward. I am urging us to ambitiously long to hear the words "Well done, good and faithful servant" (Matthew 25:23).

Paul provides fuel for our fire in 2 Timothy 2:20-21: "In a large house there are articles not only of gold and silver, but also of wood and clay; some are for special purposes and some for common use. *Those who cleanse themselves from the latter will be instruments for special purposes, made holy, useful to the Master and prepared to do any good work.*"

Notice that in order to position ourselves to be used by God in the broadest capacity, we must first *cleanse* ourselves (v.21). This is repentance. If we are ambitious to be used for any purpose God desires, we must start by removing the figurative wood and clay.

The wood and clay represent things in our lives which impede our progress in the faith. It will require a heart of wisdom to discern the wood and clay in your life, and will best be accomplished through prayer, in agreement with the word of God, and with the help of trusted and mature believers.

Our pride and ignorance blinds us from seeing the depths of our depravity, but that doesn't mean we should fail to consistently invite God to perform heavenly-sized house cleanings.

The passage above leads me to consider several questions. First, why would we desire anything less than to be an instrument for *special purposes* (v.21)?

We tend to live our lives based on our desires, which often determine the arc of our future. Our appropriate desire as children of the High King should be to move ourselves into a position where we can be used by God for *any* task he may assign us. This is a righteous desire, and it should be a controlling desire in our lives.

In reality, we are free to desire God in the very depths of our being. We temporarily content ourselves with desires for boyfriends or girlfriends, nice cars or boats, substantial savings accounts, or a name for ourselves within our profession. What should stop us from passionately desiring to be instruments God uses to bring truth to a lost world? Quite simply, NOTHING. There is no law against seeking first the kingdom of God.

Secondly, how can we justify remaining in our current state of spiritual development when the promise of being *made holy* (v.21) is available?

The beauty of walking in holiness before the Most High should both awe and inspire us to push forward. As believers we have been plucked from the eternal fire, which is the common destiny of lost souls, and have been placed in a position of favor with God. We have been set apart for God and are being made holy. He has promised to work all things for our good, and He is faithfully committed to crafting us into the image of Jesus Christ.

For the remainder of our lives, God will be transforming us into the image of Christ. We will radiate His image throughout the eons of eternity. This is no time to sit on your inheritance. There is no scriptural justification for choosing to remain on the sidelines and wait out your predestined end.

Full throttle is the speed limit of heaven. Yesterday is history, and today is our opportunity to know God and become the man or woman he desires us to become. I do not know what motivates you, but becoming a man or woman of intense intimacy with Christ and serving before Him as a priest should thrill your spirit. Status quo has got to go.

And finally, what believer in their right mind would desire anything less than being *prepared to do any good work* (v.21)? This is where godly ambition finds fulfillment – working through the power of God, in the presence of God, for the glory of God.

What an unspeakable honor! We should be the most driven people on the face of the planet. We should desire to excel in the things of God. Passion for the things of God should consume us, and it should be evident to everyone around us.

Who says we should hold back from seeking to be in the middle of a move of God? Who says we should content ourselves with the ignoble when the noble is available? The opportunity to gain the best has been given, so lead the way in seeking it, and not for your own glory, but to please His precious heart.

Of this you can be assured, unless you repent of a lackadaisical and smug approach to eternity you will never ambitiously seek to excel in your preparation for eternity. We must ask our Father to forgive us for a casual, take-life-for-granted mindset, and replace it with a singular focus to live the remainder of our days ambitiously preparing to meet Christ. We must go big or go home.

At the end of each chapter I hope to share a little encouragement with you to help motivate you to make the Divine Investment on a daily basis. As a middle-school teacher of mine once said, this is the point where I get to "clear a spot and pitch a fit."

In this chapter we have seen that repentance is not only the first step in acquiring salvation, but is also a necessary and powerful discipline in the life of a believer. I have challenged you to consider the wisdom of acquiring godly ambition, so that you will not ultimately sabotage or limit your potential to prepare for eternity. To those ends, please take the following to heart when you ponder whether you are ready to change the way you think about life and eternity.

It does not matter what age you are, set your mind on things above right now. It doesn't matter if your parents or friends fail to encourage you to seek God. Seek Him now.

It doesn't matter one bit what you have done before with your life, this is your present and great opportunity. The Most High God has given you the liberty to hunger and thirst for his righteousness, hunger for Him now.

Christ has set you free so that you can experience *exactly what you were made for* and no one has the power to keep you from seeing it come to pass. You are empowered by the hand that crafted the flower, the shark, the stars, and you are more beautiful and precious to Him than any of them. Seize your inheritance! It is waiting on the other side of the door of repentance.

You and you alone will stand on that great day when the movie of your life is played before your eyes in the presence of Christ, and you alone will answer for your obedience. Excuses will hold no weight in judgment. By God's grace, you have His power within to see that the film is glorious.

Time can become your friend. You can use time to see God move in you and around you. You will play a part as he moves people and nations closer to Him. He knew you before you were born. He chose you before He created the earth. His Son was crucified so that you can know Him, receive His love, and take His words to the ends of the earth. Your greatest end, by the grace of God, cannot be denied.

Ask God to change your mind about the way you see life, and the way you see eternity. Pray that God makes the ultimate reality of your eternal existence an ever-present reality in your daily life. Beg Him to alert you when opportunities to minister present themselves, and when the chance to store up treasures is laid before you.

Seek to associate with others who have their minds set on seeking Christ. Refuse to follow the example of lukewarm and apathetic Christians, even if they are in leadership positions. Do not be lulled to sleep by the love of things that will not cross the great divide into eternity.

You can be a world-changer as the world-changer changes you. Step up to the plate and swing away. Go Big!

CHAPTER 3
MAKING DIFFICULT DECISIONS:
THE CALL TO ABANDONMENT

They say the proof of the pudding is in the eating. Similarly, the proof of your repentance is in your willingness to abandon the things you have repented of. In abandonment, a measure of pain is often required so that we may be fashioned more perfectly into the image of Christ. It is a place between the hammer and the anvil.

Abandonment is not a pleasant word for those who are content with a comfortable lifestyle. Nevertheless, it is a calling and command we have received from our Lord. Christ unequivocally stated "those of you who do not give up everything you have cannot be my disciples" (Luke 14:33).

It is mandatory that a disciple abandon ownership of everything he has to Christ. There is no middle ground for a half-hearted commitment. It's all or nothing.

This challenge and declaration has reverberated through the halls of my heart since I began to follow Christ as an adult. At a minimum, it means we must place everything we have at the disposal of Christ. Nothing we are, nothing we have, can come before Christ.

This demand includes not only our possessions, but also our bodies, relationships, minds, wills, and time. The all-or-nothing nature of the calling to fortify your repentance by abandonment is why I have entitled this chapter *Making Difficult Decisions*.

The progression from repentance to abandonment is straightforward: After we repent of every attitude and behavior which hinders us in our preparation to stand before Christ, we must abandon those particular attitudes and behaviors so that new ones may be adopted in their place.

While this process may not appear glamorous or appetizing, repentance and abandonment ultimately break up the fallow ground of our hearts so that we may sow eternal seeds in the lives of others. We discard the unproductive and temporary so we may invest in the fruitful and eternal.

All the while, this beautiful process is marked by the relentless love of God and the humble surrender of all we have to His will. Although this process entails virtually every aspect of our lives, three areas are particularly significant.

ABANDONING OUR WILL

The human will is the command center where the choices of life are made. Because the will pulls the trigger on the actions we take, it is vital that our wills be subjected to Christ and abandoned to His greater purposes. If we cannot get past our will and our way, we cannot proceed with Him along the path of His will and His ways.

Paul taught us that it is God "who works in you to will and to act in order to fulfill his good purpose" (Philipians 2:13). God literally moves within you to help you make decisions which further His purposes. Unfortunately, our sinful nature often obstructs His work by leading us to make decisions based on our own designs and purposes. Still, He is constantly working to help us move our wills aside and make the decisions and choices He would have us make.

What a blessed will He has for you if only you will let go of your own! Those who have consistently submitted to the will of the Father know from experience that His will is flawless and beautiful in all it brings into being.

If God is leading you to abandon a pursuit or path, a job, a toy, or a relationship, then by wisdom let go of your plan and embrace his will. You will be proven much the wiser, and His infinite wisdom will be proven much superior to yours.

Christ provided the perfect example of an abandoned will. First, Christ willfully chose to be obedient to His Father's desire for Him to come to earth and die for our sins. Christ stated "I have not come on my own; God sent me" (John 8:42).

The Father told the Son to go, and the Son appeared in Mary's womb. This abandonment of His will to that of the Father continued until His last breath on the cross, and was on its greatest display in the garden when He prayed "not my will, but yours be done" (Luke 22:42). If our Lord saw fit to live His entire life in perfect submission to the will of the Father, how much more then should we?

Although we have no way of imagining what great gifts God will bring to the world through the abandonment of our wills, we do know these gifts will be more than we could ever cook up for ourselves. The challenge for us is to reach a place in our relationship with Christ where, by habitually surrendering our will to His, we learn "to test and approve what God's will is – his good, pleasing and perfect will" (Romans 12:2).

You may have to leave a place of leadership, recognition, honor, or power, but His call to abandonment is your power to obey. Get up and go!

Secondly, Christ abandoned the notion that he should rely upon His own strength to do the work of God, and chose to move in the strength of His Father. He openly acknowledged His humble dependence upon His father by stating "By myself I can do nothing . . . for I seek not to please myself but him who sent me" (John 5:30).

How often we begin in our own strength, proceed in our own strength, and ultimately fail in our own strength! This is not the pattern Christ modeled.

As the student is no greater than his master, we must recognize our tendency to habitually move in our own strength, and abandon this habit. We must humble ourselves and seek to proceed in His strength.

Like Christ, we will experience the strength of the Father if we stop asserting our sufficiency, and with humility rely upon the intervention of the Holy Spirit. It is "not by might nor by power, but by my Spirit, says the Lord" (Zechariah 4:6).

Christ also submitted His will to his Father in the

miracles and works He accomplished. In John 14:10 Jesus stated "It is the Father, living in me, who is doing his work." God the Father was moving and working through the perfectly submitted will of Christ. It is no wonder Christ was able to say "I always do what pleases Him" (John 8:29).

God wants us to experience a habitual, continual, and complete death to self so that He can move and work in us. When God moves and works in us we too will do "what pleases Him."

Finally, Christ abandoned His will to the Father by allowing the Father to choose the very words He spoke. Notice in John 12:49 Christ stated "I did not speak on my own, but the Father who sent me commanded me to say all that I have spoken." Again, in verse 50 he stated "Whatever I say is just what the Father has told me to say."

When Jesus was speaking, the Father was speaking. This teaches us that a submitted will includes a submitted tongue. Peter urged us along this same path by stating "If anyone speaks, they should do so as one who speaks the very words of God" (I Peter 4:11).

What emerges from the life of Christ is a clear picture of the life God desires for each of us. Christ abandoned His will to the Father and obediently came to earth, moved only in the strength of His Father, did only the works His Father told him to do, spoke only the words His Father told him to speak, and ultimately died the death the Father willed for Him to die.

Will you decide to go where God calls, relying on His strength as you go, and do what He desires as you speak His words? We must abandon our wills to the will of the Father if we are to accomplish His purposes. Only then will we be able to properly invest the remaining years of our lives in the boundless eons of eternity.

ABANDONING OUR TIME

If Christ is Lord over everything in your life, then Christ is Lord of your time. Turn off your phone for a few minutes and pull your high speed train into the station for a bit.

Pretend you are monk in a monastery, or a nun in a cloister, and don't be afraid of a small dose of biblical contemplation. Take some time to consider how you view time. Do you submit your daily schedule to Christ? Is Christ your time manager?

If you are to make the most of every opportunity, then you must abandon the false notions that time belongs to you, that you are to be in control of how you spend your time, and that you are lord over your time and your schedule.

What we call *our time* is, in reality, *His time* on loan to us. Once again, when it comes to a biblical understanding of time, we find ourselves in a position of stewardship rather than ownership.

Reflect upon the consequences of seeing the minutes of your life as precious gifts from God, to be used by God for God. If you lay down your supposed ownership and management of time at the feet of Jesus, then you will begin to see how He can use this precious currency to bring the Kingdom of God to bear, both in your life and in the lives of those around you.

God takes the ordinary and makes it extraordinary. A common scenario looks something like the following. First, we are convicted by God to spend some time with Him, or to engage in some type of ministry. We mull the opportunity over and begin at once to talk ourselves out of doing it, exerting our creative energy in devising reasons why we should simply avoid taking the time.

Next, after realizing our solid arguments against the task at hand are poorly disguised excuses for not doing what we know to be right, we reluctantly agree to do what God has called us to do. Then, assuming we had a good attitude, we come to realize the once dreaded activity was indeed a gift from God, a divine use of our time.

Finally, seeing we were able to take part in a work of God, and once again being reminded that "it is greater to give than receive," we give thanks to God and wonder why we ever resist His leadership.

No matter how frequently this cycle repeats itself, we still remain gun-shy to commit time to ministry. Alas, in the end we tend to be habitual time-hoarders. We need to abandon our self-service mentality about time and view time as the God-given forum for eternally significant events.

Christ stated "The Son of Man did not come to be served, but to serve" (Mark 10:45). To redeem the time our focus should be turned away from pleasing ourselves and onto serving Christ and accomplishing His purposes.

When we begin to view time as a precious chance to serve others, we will be set free from the slavish control of a self-serving lifestyle, and eternity will bear witness to how He salvaged our time for His glory.

Oh, the power of handing the keys of our time over to Christ! I would not have accomplished one good work in Christ over the past 15 years had I not allowed Him to take my time and make the best of it. And I dare not guess what was lost when I failed to abandon my time for his greater purposes. I challenge you to lay your calendar at the feet of Jesus and give Him absolute freedom to reorganize it according to what He thinks best.

It is said that the longest journey begins with a single step. Look over the pattern of your life and how you spend "your" time. Analyze the amount of time you spend pursuing leisure, the way you rigorously demand that you accomplish this or that goal in a given day, or the amount of time you spend working when you should be at home with the kids.

Take some time to simply ask God how He would have you rearrange your schedule to allow Him to have a greater presence in your daily life, and expect a quick answer. Once you abandon your supposed ownership of time, Christ will find time in your schedule to place you in the middle of the movement of God, and often demand instant and unplanned obedience, which is the topic of our next chapter.

ABANDONING OUR POSSESSIONS

Finally, we must understand that Jesus is Lord of our possessions, and abandon the incorrect belief that we have the right to do with them as we please. Psalms 24:1 states "The earth is the Lord's, and everything in it." On its face, this passage means everything you have already belongs to God. His name is on the title deed of the universe, and that deed includes your possessions and mine. We are merely stewards of the possessions of God.

The truth of God's ownership presses us to analyze whether we view our possessions as ours for our purposes or as His for His purposes. Once we wrap our minds around the biblically indisputable fact that God is the true owner of our possessions, we will begin to see them as being placed in trust with us so that He can direct us to use them as He wills.

As this picture of God's ownership emerges, abandonment comes more clearly into focus. We no longer have the right to do what we please with our money and toys, but should earnestly seek to be found faithful in our duty as stewards. The call of Christ to abandon everything to Him no longer appears to be a radical command, but rather a head's-up from a loving Father to his children to step out of the fairy tale and into reality.

Abandonment of our possessions is an act of faith which acknowledges the overarching truth that all we have belongs to God and is to be governed solely by His will, not ours. When you let go, you illustrate your belief that God is big enough to be trusted to "meet all your needs" according to his riches (Philipians 4:19).

Practically, this means we have to let go of things we prize so we may invest them as God desires. Whether this means retaining our possessions or selling them, they must be placed on God's chopping block and committed to Him, the rightful owner. Whatever the King wants us to abandon, we abandon, and whatever the King wants us to keep, we keep. He is the Lord. He makes the calls. We merely follow His marching orders.

In conclusion, we must make difficult decisions if we are to move forward in Christ. We must repent of the notion we own and are in control of our will, our time, and our possessions.

Following up on repentance by abandoning the lifestyle we are comfortable with will require change, daily discipline, and accountability. When our pursuit of pleasure and leisure rear their ugly head in the face of a call to abandonment, spiritual warfare will ensue. Your fleshly nature will war against your naked exposure to the will of God. However, make no mistake, you will not fully invest yourself in eternity without allowing the call to abandonment to permeate the decision-making processes of your daily life.

Is Jesus worth it to you? Is the Most High worthy of your willful abandonment of your decisions, your time, your possessions? Are you willing to toss overboard the dead weight in order to stay afloat on the current of God's will?

All the honor creation can yield is infinitely inferior to the honor He deserves. Let go! Turn loose! Abandon it all to Christ. His Word and your faith tell you there are rewards awaiting your move.

If there is a call to abandonment, then there is a call to blessing in abandonment. Don't cheat yourself out of eternal riches for the temporal gratification of your toys and habits. There is no need to stumble in the front stretch of the race.

You have repented of a casual indifference to the things of eternity, so solidify your position and jettison your junk. Let go of anything which holds you back or slows you down in your pursuit of the eternally perfect and good plan of God for your life. The time for holding on has come and gone.

If we have Christ, we have enough. It was Saint Patrick who prayed: "Christ with me, Christ before me, Christ behind me, Christ in me, Christ beneath me, Christ above me, Christ on my right, Christ on my left, Christ where I lie, Christ where I sit, Christ where I arise, Christ in the heart of everyone who thinks of me, Christ in the mouth of everyone who speaks to me, Christ in every eye that sees me, Christ in every ear that hears me."

Christ is our life, our hope, and our greatest end. We position ourselves to fully attain His blessings only when we thoroughly abandon our wills, our time, and our possessions to His lordship.

CHAPTER 4
THE POWER OF YES:
THE CALL TO OBEDIENCE

Hopefully, at this point you have admitted the need for a change in focus, and have repented of a small-time, earth-bound way of thinking. You have decided to go big for God and the trajectory of your life has begun to change. After refocusing your life on your eternal destiny, you have prayerfully considered what this practically means for your life.

Most likely, God has shown you a thing or two you need to throw overboard, and you have abandoned your stranglehold on your will, your time, and your possessions. Now, you must train yourself to habitually say *yes* to God.

In a nutshell, this chapter will cover *why* we should obey, and the remainder of the book will offer scriptural principles regarding *how* to obey.

"Thou shalt not" has a haunting ring to most of us, and its brother "thou shalt" likewise fails to warm our hearts. We instinctively bristle at being told what to do. We are much more comfortable asserting our own will and following our own paths. We prefer to choose for ourselves, no matter how small or how great the question. Fortunately, this attitude meets certain death when we walk in simple obedience to the commands of Christ.

God has shown over and over throughout human history that He enjoys displaying His power through the humble obedience of His servants. Recall Abraham saying *yes* by ushering Isaac to the altar of sacrifice, Moses saying *yes* by demanding Pharoah let his people go, and David saying *yes* to the challenge to face Goliath in the Valley of Elah.

God challenged our spiritual fathers in unique ways and

in unique settings, but the call to obey was always the same. Our plight is not unlike those who have gone before us. "The eyes of the Lord range throughout the earth to strengthen those whose hearts are fully committed to Him" (2 Chronicles 16:9). God is still looking for humble men and women to do what He says so He can show Himself great among the nations.

Don't be surprised when God challenges you to do things you would not have imagined. Like the ancients, you will be forced to choose between obedience and disobedience. With each command you will experience either the power and blessing of *yes* or the loss and failure of *no*. The great men and women of God in scripture said *yes* to the commands of God: so must you.

God has plans for you. When you say *yes* you unleash upon Earth the great power and eternal potential of those plans. Now is your time to obey and leave a legacy of obedience for those that follow. Today is the day for you to see the power of God moving through your every *yes*. In Heaven the tale of what He accomplished through your obedience will be retold to His glory.

WHY WE SHOULD OBEY

My pastor has taught me that in order to build conviction we must teach *why* things are as they are. This principle is strikingly true when it comes to answering the question of why we should say yes to God.

To obey means to submit, and before we submit we tend to want good reasons for our submission. After all, based on all the reliable evidence I have seen or heard, we did not bargain for our existence: We were created, placed here, and told to obey the will of an unseen God.

As a young man, I wrestled for three years with this existential dilemma after watching my aunt pass away from cancer amidst a hailstorm of prayers from our community. Gayle Lowe was the life of the party, full of energy, smiling and laughing with her echoing, boisterous laugh. She was the choir director at her church, and one of my best and most faithful friends.

Gayle developed cancer in late Spring of 1993, and died in the fall of the same year. I often took her to chemotherapy treatments, and watched her slowly degrade into a shell of the woman she had been.

I fell apart after her death. Many gut-wrenching questions came to the surface and began to haunt me. I found myself questioning the value of prayer, the origin of evil, the legitimacy of scripture and many other questions previously considered out-of-bounds. I found no acceptable answers. I began to develop an unspoken hatred for God which eventually spilled over into outright rebellion.

After three years of traveling down this track I found myself utterly confused, hopeless, and miserable. I quit my job in Northern Virginia, withdrew my 401k, and determined to move to the Pacific Northwest to end my days in an unbridled stampede of debauchery. It was at this point that I received a life-changing letter from my mom.

In her letter she recounted the various stages of my life and how, through it all, her only desire had been that I would know God and do His will. From a feeling of indebtedness to her I purposed to allow two weeks to give a last look at what the Bible had to say about these questions.

I will never forget the moment, sometime near the end of this two week period, when I was sitting on my knees in my condo reading scripture. All at once, I sat up and the words came from the depths of my soul like the whisper of God passing before Elijah, "Jesus Christ is the Son of God." The answer to why I should obey was given.

It was a simple truth that demanded my ultimate allegiance. Although I was still unable to understand why my aunt passed away, why we pray, or how Lucifer became Satan, obedience to Christ became the high calling of my life.

The threshold question of *why* we should obey is answered in the God-Man, Jesus Christ. We strain and struggle, question and explore, and in the end are led to the singular revelation that faith in Christ is required to know and understand God.

Reason ushers us to the door of Christ, and we enter through faith. Once we are in Christ and come to know the *Who* of God, we begin to progressively inherit the riches of the mystery of the *Why* of God. God has revealed at least three powerful reasons why we should obey Him, so let us look at them together.

HIS GLORY

"You are worthy, our Lord and God, to receive glory and honor and power, for you created all things, and by your will they were created and have their being" (Revelation 4:11). God demands our obedience so that His name will be glorified through our obedience.

He chose to create us and place us here, and even now He chooses to sustain our every breath. All glory belongs to Him, and a huge part of our role in this grand drama is to simply allow Him to reflect His glory through us as we humbly submit in obedience to His commands.

God will ultimately bring every act, every word, and every created being into judgment, and the wisdom of His commands will be exhibited for all to see. His glory will be magnified throughout all of eternity.

"I am the Lord; that is my name! I will not yield my glory to another" (Isaiah 42:8). You may bristle at the thought of God being so deeply interested in His glory. This may strike you as the ultimate dish of self-service. It may even be an unspoken hindrance to your desire to obey God.

Quite frankly, I choked on this pill for quite a while. I could not fathom why God cared so much about upholding His reputation among His created munchkins, when we were not necessary to His existence in the first place.

Ultimately, two thoughts emerged from this issue. First, the sobering reality is we will likely never grasp the full depth of the answer to this mystery. Some things are simply beyond our reach.

The Apostle Paul spoke of a heavenly law which renders certain eternal mysteries inexpressible. Notice how in 2

Corinthians 12:4 the visitor to the third heaven "heard inexpressible things, things that no one is permitted to tell." It appears from this scripture that there are things too great for human words.

Although intellectual curiosity will often lead you to questions beyond your ability to answer, there is no need to let the unknown stifle your growth. You know the One who holds the unknown – the Supreme Lawgiver who determines what we may or may not speak about. Sometimes our duty is to simply hold on to what we know is true until our Father decides to bring us into a deeper revelation of who He is and why we are here.

Second, the truth of the matter is HE DESERVES GLORY! The very justice of God, which we are told is the foundation of his throne, righteously demands that all glory belong to Him. Because God is who He is, He could never demand anything less than every single ounce of glory in the entire universe throughout all of eternity. For any other creature, whether it be Lucifer or your neighbor, to attempt to take from His glory would be eternal thievery, cosmic treason.

It is right that God demands all glory, and it is right that we seek to give Him *ALL* the glory. God has proven He is worthy to receive all glory by the witness of his wonderful creation, by the innate way in which we *know* He exists, by his patient dealings with the saints, and ultimately through the revelation of Himself in Christ.

He also shows us His glory during times of worship. In the story of the woman at the well, Christ taught that the Father actively seeks true worshippers (John 12:23). When we worship Him in Spirit and in truth we glorify God.

In worship we experience an indescribable longing to see His face and to be with Him throughout eternity. Surely you have experienced those moments when you wished you had 1,000 tongues to praise Him, and it seemed that having 1,000 tongues would hardly be enough to give Him what He deserved.

In worship our feet stand firmly on the bedrock reality that nothing is greater than glorifying Him, and nothing can compare to giving all we are for all He is. In worship the truth that God *ought* to receive all glory validates itself to our spirit.

When we worship, we experience how fitting it is that God be glorified. We understand how *right* it is that He be praised, and how blessed we are to merely utter a syllable of adoration toward His perfection.

Please do not misunderstand why I am encouraging you to obey God. In proposing that you make the Divine Investment, I am not proposing a way for you to seek to increase *your* glory in eternity, far from it. I am encouraging you to let go of what can be seen and take hold of what cannot *so that God will be glorified* by your obedience. Obedience is merely the righteous response to what God rightly deserves.

The entire scope of the Divine Investment is arced towards and ends with the ultimate glory of God. I am convinced if you live your life focused on eternity you will glorify the wisdom, love, and righteousness of God in far greater measure than you would otherwise.

In turn, you will enjoy life to a greater degree, which glorifies God. Also, you will ultimately be found faithful on judgment day, which glorifies God. We are not in this for our glory, but to see Him receive glory through our lives.

HIS LOVE

We should obey God not only because our obedience results in His glory, but also because He is love. His motivation in seeking our obedience will always be guided by His great love toward us. He says "I have loved you with an everlasting love" (Jeremiah 31:3).

For some unfathomable reason, God has chosen to bind Himself to us by His love. He does not command us to do things which lead us into evil, nor does He pull our strings like a puppeteer. He does not command us to repent, abandon, and obey because He derives pleasure from our pain. On the contrary, His great love moves Him to give us commands which, when followed, result in our protection, peace, and spiritual prosperity.

"I know the plans I have for you, declares the Lord, plans to prosper you and not to harm you, plans to give you hope and a future" (Jeremiah 29:11). God has great plans for us!

There is no reason to fear what might happen if we obey Him. There is no reason to doubt the motivation behind His commands, or to assume even for a moment some ill-intent behind His directives. Even when we cannot understand why, we can rest in this assurance: God is coming to us from a place of love, commanding us in love, and looking to guard our way in love.

This beautiful truth frees us to strike forward in obedience as conquerors in the Kingdom of God. If God is leading you to take a step of faith, then rest assured His love is leading you to take that step of faith.

If you are questioning why God says you should not go a certain direction, then rest assured His love is attempting to lead you onto the right path and spare you the pain, guilt, and shame of a wrong turn. There is no biblical basis to believe otherwise: To move forward in obedience to His will is to live a life encircled by and infused with His love.

The difficult part of the equation is determining what the will of God may be in a certain matter. Paul helps us with this question in Romans chapter 12. In verses 1 and 2 we are told to offer our bodies as a living sacrifice to God (abandonment), and to allow our minds to be transformed by thinking in new ways (repentance). He then shares with us the result of obedience: "*then* you will be able to test and approve what God's will is, His good, pleasing, and perfect will" (emphasis mine).

As we repent of our old ways of thinking and abandon ourselves to His service, we develop the ability to discern His will. As we discern and obey His will, we are led to an even greater knowledge and experience of his loving plan for us. This process is what I call a "divine cycle." With every step of obedience our lives open like a flower to the sunshine our Father.

Imagine a loving parent calling his child to come into a room just around the corner so the child may receive a surprise from the parent. The duty of the child, if he hopes to receive the surprise, is to walk around the corner and into the room. If the child disobeys, the child may never receive the surprise.

It is like this with our Father. He has more surprises around the corner than we could ever imagine, but we must walk around the corner to receive them. I encourage you: trust that what *He* has for you is greater than what *you* have for you.

TO DEMONSTRATE OUR LOVE

The third reason we should obey God is because we love Him. Jesus pointedly stated, "If you love me, keep my commands" (John 14:15). We prove our love for God by our obedience, and disprove our professed love for God by our disobedience. Despite the bluntness and discomfort, we must face this truth head-on and come to terms with its application to our lives.

At first blush, this verse was very offensive to me. I felt I was merely a pawn in a cosmic game of chess. However, after years of reflection, I now believe the reason why this passage struck me so negatively was because it offended my pride. It restricted my ability to call my own shots.

Somewhere between John Wayne and Captain America, I was taught to depend upon myself, to create an image of myself which exudes strength and independence. But in this passage self-reliance is slammed against the rocks, and replaced by utter and complete dependence upon Jesus.

Christ has called our bluff. The test of true love is obedience. We can speak of our love, or we can prove it by our obedience. Love for God must necessarily translate into obedience to His commands.

We cannot say we love God and then forsake obedience. No amount of sacrifice, good deeds, or pleasant smiles can substitute for obedience. If we say we love him, we should obey Him.

I have come to understand this passage in part because I too am a father, and have experienced this truth many times with my children. Even though I am a loving father and tell my kids to do things because I love them, they sometimes fail to obey me. I, in turn, am hurt by their disobedience.

It appears Christ was expressing a similar sentiment when he lamented over Jerusalem, saying "How often I have longed to gather your children together, as a hen gathers her chicks under her wings, and you were not willing" (Matthew 23:37). May we seek His strength to help us avoid grieving His spirit within us (Ephesians 4:30).

Let's look at a common scenario. First, God commands us to do certain things out of His infinite love and concern for our well-being, knowing that it will be good for us if we obey. In response, we sometimes fail to obey a black-and-white command of scripture, or fail to follow the leadership of His Spirit. In the end, our loving Father is rejected by the disobedience of His obstinate child. We see this scenario played out over and over in his dealings with Israel, and, if we are honest, in ourselves.

I challenge you to accept the call to obedience not as a affront to your pride, or as a ploy of a God bent on manipulation, but rather as the heartfelt cry of a loving God beckoning His precious children to obey His loving commands.

Many mysteries surrounding our existence remain unsolved, but Christ made certain there is no mystery as to how to please Him. If we truly love our God, our desire will be to please Him, and our desire to please Him will lead us to obey Him. Our love for God finds its perfect fulfillment when we say *yes* to God.

Know that your love of God will move you to obey even when it is painful, scary, or uncomfortable. Know that your life will inevitably be marked by submission to the leadership of the Holy Spirit if your love is true. Do not be surprised when you find yourself in situations you never would have imagined.

Prayerfully look at your life, and with the help of others isolate areas where God may be urging you to take a step of obedience, then get moving. Let your love for God move you like a locomotive along the tracks of simple obedience to his promptings.

THE POWER OF OBEDIENCE

In conclusion, allow me to remind you that the power of obedience has been used by God to create the stories, unlock the unlimited, reveal the unsearchable, and save souls. Enoch was whooshed away in a flash. Noah built an ark and saved the human race. Abraham drew a knife on his son and became the spiritual father of all believers. Moses stood between God and Israel.

Joshua saw the wall of Jericho fall. Samuel anointed kings. Isaiah and the prophets saw into the heavenly realms. Three Israelite boys walked into the mouth of a furnace. And in the ultimate act of obedience, Jesus Christ died on a cross to save your soul.

John witnessed the end of the world. Peter was crucified upside down. Martin Luther said "Here I stand." John Wycliffe gave us an English bible. Charles Finney blazed with the Spirit. Mother Teresa reached down, and the hopeless looked up. Watchman Knee died alone in prison, and Billy Graham shouted to the whole world.

The power of God has been displayed in every generation through the simple obedience of his humble servants. You too have a part to play in this cosmic drama.

What will be said of you at the end of your days? Did you stand on the shores of disobedience or did you travel on the wonderful river of the will of God? Did you casually dismiss the will of God in what appeared to be insignificant choices, or did you say yes to that quiet voice and take part as God wrote another beautiful chapter in His book of life?

God demands our obedience and we must give it. The Divine Investment is propelled by obedience, but is slowed by disobedience. Obey quickly. Obey in confidence. Obey though it cost you all you have.

CHAPTER 5
AWAITING ORDERS:
THE CALL TO ABIDE

"To the left . . . to the left . . . to the left, right, left" echoes the drill sergeant as his soldiers march in step. They listen to his commands and follow them with precision, stepping how and when they are told. The steps of the soldiers are much like your obedience to the commands of God: You step when and where you are told.

Now, let's picture the soldiers just before the drill sergeant issues his first order. They stand at attention, their posture erect, their uniforms crisp, their ears perked for the voice of the sergeant. They are awaiting orders.

In the same way, as a soldier in the army of God it is your duty to stand at attention and await your orders. You are to place yourself in a posture of attention before your Commander. This is done by *abiding in Christ.*

As we have learned thus far in our quest to make the Divine Investment, we must let go of our old views and lifestyles by repentance and abandonment, and we must say yes to the commands of God. As we obey, God glorifies Himself as His power is unleashed in our lives, and we are ushered onto a path greater than any we could have imagined.

It's time now to establish your spiritual posture for executing the Divine Investment. In this journey of life, you move forward by abiding in the presence of Christ. As you abide in Him, he will produce spiritual fruit inside you, and propel you to accomplish good works which will survive the fires of judgment.

ABIDING IN CHRIST

"Abide in me, and I in you" (John 15:4, KJV). Abiding in Christ is both a moment-by-moment recognition of the presence of God, and a continual submission of your will to the leadership of the Holy Spirit within. It is a living and fluid fellowship with the Father, Son, and Spirit, bought by the blood of Christ.

As you remain in the awareness of the presence of Christ, He produces spiritual fruit within you, and propels you to do the good works He desires to accomplish through you. Seen as such, abiding is a divine honor, and a discipline which you have the privilege of practicing.

The challenge to abide was one of the first challenges Christ issued to me as a young believer. One night as I was walking through the woods mediating on John 15:4, Christ spoke to me and said, "Abide in me" (KJV). Though His words were inaudible, His voice was clear and unmistakable. His words that night prompted me to begin the lifelong pursuit of abiding, and this pursuit has admittedly been the most difficult challenge of my life.

In order to understand abiding, we need to distinguish our *position* of being in Christ and our *practice* of abiding in Christ. Positionally, God chose us to be *in Him* before the foundation of the world (Ephesians 1:4). As God's dearly loved children, we belong to Christ, and no one can snatch us from the Father's hand (John 10:29). Our lives have been hidden with Christ in God (Ephesians 3:3). God sees us as His treasured possession, and has prepared a place for us to dwell with Him for all of eternity (Matthew 25:34). Therefore, we are secure in our position in Christ.

Despite our position in Christ, we often fail to *practice* the discipline of choosing to abide in Christ. Our sinful human nature, the world, and all the heavenly forces of darkness wage war against the Spirit of God within us, and against the expression of the life of Christ through us.

We are literally locked in an age-old war between Christ and his enemies, and because we are in Christ and allied with Him, His enemies have their sights set on us. It is not a twisted joke, a fairy tale, or science fiction: We "fight against the rulers, against the authorities, against the powers of this dark world and against the spiritual forces of evil in the heavenly realms" (Ephesians 6:12) which desire to destroy us, our families, our churches, and our nation.

The result of the war raging around us and in our bodies is that we often act or react in ungodly ways and fail to allow Christ to live through us. Rather than moving in the power of the Holy Spirit, we often move in our own power and fail miserably.

We often grow impatient, act in anger, focus on the things of this world, and spend considerable amounts of time dimly aware of the presence of God. In effect, we choose to allow the flesh to manifest itself in us, rather than allowing Christ to manifest Himself in us.

This does not have to be the case, for "sin shall no longer be your master" (Romans 6:14). We must learn to abide in Christ if we are to see the power of Christ move through us in triumph over the deadly enemies of the world, the flesh, and the devil.

Now that we have established the difference between our position and our practice, we must take a brief detour to dispense with a common misconception Satan uses to wreak havoc in the body of Christ. The misconception lies in a belief that victory in the Christian life is somehow gained by our effort *for* God, or our zeal *for* His cause, rather than through His power *in* us.

It is a dangerous myth, historically assumed by both young and old, that we are to suit up as a knight, mount our steed, and charge headlong into the battle under the banner of the cross to gain victory for our king. On the contrary, scripture teaches that victory is "not by might, nor by power, but by my Spirit says the Lord" (Zechariah 4:6).

Sometimes a small preposition makes a huge difference. In this case, the focus is on the *in* rather than the *for*. The scripture does not read "you *for* Christ," but "Christ *in* you" (Colossians 1:27, italics mine). It must be established in our hearts and minds that our position and power are *in* Christ, and that we follow His lead to victory.

Far from choosing when, where, and how to do God's work and merely asking Christ to come along with us, when we abide in Christ, He leads. He moves us according to *His* will, in *His* power, and in *His* time and ways. He accomplishes His purposes through us as we submit ourselves to be used by Him. In fact and in practice we resemble the steed much more than the knight.

When we grasp the subtle yet profound distinction that our power is *in, by, and through* Christ, we will be motivated to take hold of the power of abiding. A clear view of our dependency will compel and energize us to habitually discipline ourselves to be aware of His presence and in tune with His desires.

We will no longer feel a need to devise ingenious plans to conquer the world, or craft creative ways to be great for God. We will see the beauty and simplicity in simply abiding and awaiting orders, and his strength will be perfected in our weakness.

SPIRITUAL FRUIT

"He that abideth in me and I in him, the same bringeth forth much fruit" (John 15:5, KJV). Spiritual fruit is an inevitable by-product of abiding in Christ. When discussing spiritual fruit, we need to remember that the term *fruit* is merely an analogy. When Christ refers to *spiritual fruit* he is using an earthly item (fruit) to create a word picture which expresses a divine character quality. As we will see, the analogy is incredibly powerful.

The fruit of the Spirit is the character which Christ perfectly exhibited and desires to produce and exhibit within us. The fruit is manifested as "love, joy, peace, forbearance, kindness, goodness, faithfulness, gentleness and self-control" (Galatians 5:22). These are the pristine and inestimably valuable by-products of abiding, the naturally occurring harvest of the life of Christ inside you.

Why is it so important that we exhibit spiritual fruit? Christ taught fruit is evidence of discipleship, and that it is to His Father's glory that we bear much fruit (John 15:8). As our lives exhibit spiritual fruit, we remind the world of the reality of Christ.

In a very real sense, the person of Christ Himself ministers love to us and to others as His love lives within us. When we exhibit self-control we illustrate to the world that we are controlled by another. When joy springs up in the midst of our worst trials, the world is reminded that there is more to this life than temporary happiness. The presence of fruit illustrates the presence of Christ in the person.

To understand how a wayward human being bears spiritual fruit, we must grasp the sequence of John 15:4-5, which reads "Abide in me, and I in you. As the branch cannot bear fruit of itself, except it abide in the vine; no more can ye, except ye abide in me. I am the vine, ye are the branches: He that abideth in me, and I in him, the same bringeth forth much fruit: for without me ye can do nothing."

Try to picture a branch of a grapevine lying on the ground. It is disconnected, decaying, and severed from its life source. It has no hope of producing more grapes. Soon it will wither, waste away, and never produce fruit again.

Now, imagine Christ is the vine, and the branch is someone without Christ. That person is no longer connected to Christ; they are severed from their life source and decaying. Christ used this analogy to teach us the importance of abiding in Him.

If we are to bear spiritual fruit we must remain attached to Christ. We must stay connected to our life source, the True Vine (John 15:1). There is no alternative if we hope to see the fruit of the Spirit spring forth upon our branch.

Consider how you are more loving, patient, and kind to your friends and family when you are aware of the presence of Christ. Then recall how irritable, impatient, and unkind you can be when you fail to walk closely with Christ. The results are quite predictable.

"Neither can you bear fruit unless you remain in me" (v.4). Apart from abiding in Christ, we have no ability to bear fruit. Pushing His point even farther, Christ bluntly stated,

"Apart from me you can do nothing" (John 15:5).

If we fail to abide in Christ, and fail to obediently submit our will to His will on a daily basis, we figuratively place ourselves in the position of the fruitless little branch – cut off, withering, dying, fruitless. The best we have to hope for apart from abiding is "nothing" (v.5).

"He that abideth in me, and I in him, the same bringeth forth much fruit" (v.5). The good news is we do not have to be the little branch lying on the ground. Far from accomplishing "nothing", Christ has promised to produce His character in us if we will abide in Him. It is a certainty of the Christian faith that we will bear fruit *IF* we abide in the vine.

If we are progressing in our love for others, and if we are becoming more patient and kind, then it is because we are abiding in Christ. On the other hand, if we are remaining stagnant or going backwards in our patience or gentleness to others, we need to refocus our lives around abiding in Christ.

<u>GOOD WORKS</u>

Christ not only expects our lives to be characterized by the fruit He produces within us, but also by the good works He accomplishes through us. A good work is any action you are moved to undertake by the Spirit of God, and accomplish by His power.

A good work can be forgiving an enemy for a wrong, helping in a local soup kitchen, telling your child a bedtime story, or sharing Christ on the street corner. Each good work is unique and has its origin in the mind of God.

"Let us move beyond the elementary teachings about Christ and be taken forward to maturity, not laying again the foundation of repentance from acts that lead to death, and of faith in God" (Hebrews 6:1). It is time we build upon the foundation of salvation by grace through faith by teaching and encouraging one another to excel in good works. Good works flow from saving faith (James 2:17) and should be a central focus of discipleship.

The scriptural references to good works are vast and

varied. What a shame to teach about salvation by faith and fail to mention the good works this salvation will produce. We need to emphasize the importance of good works, and "consider how we may spur one another on toward love and good deeds" (Hebrews 10:24).

If we repent, abandon, obey, and abide, we will no doubt be used by Christ to minister in His power. A quick glance at your nearest Christian history book will readily reveal the good works God has accomplished in his saints.

Recall Paul cutting a path for the gospel across Asia and Europe, Luther confronting the abuses of the medieval church, and Wycliffe being burned at the stake for translating the Bible into English. Or at a more intimate level, recall how someone once preached the gospel to a lost heart which was once your own.

The power of Christ within us is an unstoppable force propelling us to be his hands, his feet, and his mouthpiece in this dying world. What a transforming influence and wonderful calling is ours to enjoy!

To fully understand the role of good works in our lives, we must understand we are to work with God, through God's power, and to God's glory. First, we are to work together with God.

Paul says "we are co-workers in God's service (I Corinthians 3:9). God is on the move, and we have the high calling of being on the move with Him. Our Father, though highly exalted above the earth, is intimately involved in accomplishing his purposes on the earth. It is our task to join Him and take part with Him in a plan which is greater than our imagination.

How humbling it is to have the opportunity to know God at all, much less to have the chance to take to the fields with Him. Ours is a cosmic privilege. No wonder Paul said we are to always give ourselves "fully to the work of the Lord" (I Corinthians 15:58).

We are not to limit our participation in the Kingdom to walking an aisle at church or in a crusade, saying our prayers, reading our Bibles, and attempting to live a good and moral life. We are to be about the business of rolling up our sleeves and doing hard labor with our God.

Our lives are not to be characterized by spiritual lethargy, mental apathy, or physical comfort. We work with the One who touched the leprous, rolled a spit ball and placed it on the eyes of the blind man, and reclined on the lap of his beloved disciple. In much the same way, He will use our arms to give a hug, our feet to walk to a neighbors' house, and our mouths to speak healing words.

Secondly, we are to work through God's power. "It is God who works in you, to will and to act in order to fulfill His good purpose" (Phillipians 2:13). Just as we are to work *with* God, it is necessary to recognize that our power to work comes *through* God within.

He is the architect of good works, and He is the person energizing and empowering us to complete the works He has created us to do. We do not move with God in our own strength. We move with God in *His* strength.

Thirdly, we work to God's glory. "Let your light shine before others, that they may see your good deeds and glorify your Father in heaven" (Matthew 5:16). When we do good works with God and through His power, the end result is His glory. Bringing glory to God is the ultimate purpose of our lives, and it should delight our hearts to bring as much glory to Him as is possible.

We cannot allow Satan to hinder our willingness to do good works, or allow him to diminish their value in our eyes. If Satan succeeds, the onlookers who would normally see God at work and glorify Him will see nothing and fail to glorify Him.

Child of the kingdom, I challenge you to not be misled and undervalue the worth of your sweat equity in the Kingdom of God. If God has moved you to work, then work in his strength!

<u>JUDGMENT</u>

The purpose of this book is to encourage you to invest

your life in eternity, and to aid you in your preparation to appear before Christ unashamed in judgment. To that end, I am bound to share you with you one final aspect of good works.

Look with me in I Corinthians 3:13-15, which states "The fire will test the quality of each person's work. If what has been built survives, the builder will receive a reward. If it is burned up, the builder will suffer loss but will yet be saved-even though only as one escaping through the flames."

In this passage, which most describe as the judgment of believers, we are told that "the fire will test the quality of each person's work" (v.13). Make no mistake, "our God is a consuming fire" (Hebrews 12:29). His everlasting eyes will most definitely look upon and test your works on earth.

Far from being lost in time and space, your works are being recorded in order that they might be recalled before the very throne of Christ. This is why Paul tells us "each one should build with care" (I Corinthians 3:10). The inescapable fact of judgment, standing alone, should motivate you to reconsider how you prioritize the quality of your work in the Kingdom.

Next, we are told "if what has been built survives, the builder will receive a reward. If it is burned up, the builder will suffer loss" (v.14-15). This passage assumes we have been building, either for better or worse. It implies we are not only expected to work, but also challenges us to build as the Apostle Paul did, on nothing other than the "foundation" of Christ (I Corinthians 3:11). Christ will not condemn the works He completed in us.

Finally, we are told if our works burn up in judgment we will suffer loss, and will be saved "only as one escaping through the flames" (v.15). It is important to point out that even though the man escaping through the flames lost his works, his soul was saved. Although this man will enjoy Christ for all of eternity, he squandered the great chance to take part in works of eternal significance while on earth. He failed to make his life a divine investment.

This is a tragedy of eternal proportion. The Divine Investment is my best attempt to help you avoid being this person. God forbid we escape with our clothes singed and our houses burned behind us in judgment.

In light of the certainty of judgment, consider whether you been living as if your every work will be rewound and replayed in judgment? Are you willing to set aside any lie, habit, or sin which hinders your preparations for the inescapable review of God in judgment? Do not allow Satan to make one last stab at the glory of God in judgment by making a mockery of your work on earth.

In conclusion, allow me to speak some words of encouragement. There is nothing more pleasing than abiding in Christ. By his grace, we are miserable without him. Make it your goal to abide in Him every moment of every day until you see His face in eternity. Your focus will change, your character will change, and God will change people around you.

As we abide in Christ, we become like Christ. You are not the person you were, and you are not the person you will be. God has great designs on the very essence of what makes you *you*.

Nestle yourself deeply in the presence of God and expect that He will increasingly change you into a person radiating His image. The end result is more than your mind can fathom. Don't shortcut the process. Our destiny is to bear fruit, let's desire to bear bushels of it.

We were "created in Christ Jesus to do good works, which God prepared in advance for us to do" (Ephesians 2:10). God has already seen and prepared what He would have you do, and it is your task to play your role as He executes His plan in your life. You have been set free so that you may be set to work. You were never meant to live a life set on cruise control. Why give your heart to the pursuit of your comforts and desires when God has something greater and higher for you?

CHAPTER 6
PRACTICING THE PRACTICAL:
THE CALL TO AUTHENTICITY,
ACCOUNTABILITY, AND COMMUNITY

"Go out to the roads and country lanes and compel them to come in, so that my house will be full" (Luke 14:23). The Divine Investment is not primarily an academic pursuit executed behind the thick walls of an ivory tower. The offering of our lives as living sacrifices is a practical exercise played out in the dirt and mud of everyday life. It demands sweat and sometimes blood.

You invest in the trenches, where you encounter the lost and dying as their time on earth evaporates and their spirits march toward a certain judgment. You invest in the local church where your brothers and sisters in Christ desperately need your presence, your words of comfort and challenge. Through it all, you invest humbly and persistently in a spirit of sincerity until your number is called and you stand in review before the King of the Universe.

In this chapter we will discuss three practical necessities which, if applied, will drive you forward in your quest to make the Divine Investment. Each is time tested and proven. They are not for the squeamish or hesitant, but for the bold and committed. My prayer is that you will incorporate them quickly, consistently, and passionately, and in turn reap their rewards.

AUTHENTICITY
First, you must resolve to be authentic. You have no time for charades in your journey to forever. It is time to be real before both God and men. Perhaps you recall being in the presence of someone you would consider to be advanced in their faith, a "spiritual giant" in your estimation.

Consider how genuine they are, how humble and sincere in their speech, attentiveness, and thoughtfulness. Their authenticity disarms us and reminds us they are not putting on a show. They are "for real". When we are in their presence we naturally drop our guard and seek wisdom from them. This maturity of character is what Christ desires to see in each of us.

Take a look at the Beatitudes in Matthew 5 and note the character traits Christ applauds. It is not the power of oratory, a magnetic presence, or a fabulous voice which is praised. It is not a trim build, good looks, or a high I.Q. Rather, it is poverty of spirit, mercy, purity, a hunger for God - those rare and authentic qualities found only in those who walk closely with Christ. We must see through the satanic smoke-screen which would obscure the worth of these priceless virtues.

I must caution that authenticity comes at a great price. We are very adept at maintaining an image of having it all together, of being on top of our game. Facades come quite naturally to us. We enjoy looking in the mirror and seeing someone of standing, someone worthy of respect.

We compare ourselves to others and search for fine distinctions that elevate our character over that of others. On the other hand, authenticity dictates that you shed these prideful, childish behaviors, and it costs you the delusional security blanket by which your deceived and vain ego is warmed.

You cannot be real until you see yourself as you truly are. However, you cannot see yourself as you truly are until you drop your guard before God and confess what He already knows. Without Christ, "you are wretched, pitiful, poor, blind, and naked" (Revelation 3:17). If you possess maturity in Christ, or have accomplished anything of eternal significance, it was only through the power and grace of God.

It is best that we immediately come to terms with the reality that we are in desperate need of God. We will never discover a day on this side of eternity in which we rise to a level of independence from His grace and mercy.

Once you stomach the not-so-tasty truth of your absolute and total dependence upon Him for your every progress in the faith, you will be able to stop the charade and be real with God and others. You will be free to exhude a different kind of confidence, a confidence grounded upon your frailty and His power.

Honesty about your position in Christ will allow you to see both yourself and others from the viewpoint of your Father. In the end, others will feel comfortable to drop their guard around you and share their deepest needs, and the opportunities for you to minister Christ will multiply.

ACCOUNTABILITY

"As iron sharpens iron, so one person sharpens another" (Proverbs 27:17). As you walk in authenticity, fully aware of your weakness and dependency upon God, you will most likely see the need to make yourself accountable to others. I am defining accountability as your willful and voluntary submission to the review and correction of other believers and your church leadership. In my opinion, accountability is not just practical, it is necessary if you really desire to go full throttle with God.

In case your feathers are getting ruffled, please understand I am not advocating offloading your deepest secrets to the nearest person in the pew, nor am I saying that true accountability will develop overnight. As with our choice of a spouse or close friend, we must choose our accountability partners wisely. An accountability relationship is developed over time in the rich soil of trust and intimacy and grows to maturity only in the greenhouse of grace and mercy.

People often bristle at the thought of being accountable, because accountability requires vulnerability. As I mentioned previously, the ideal of manhood in our society is a self-made, self-reliant man. Vulnerability flies in the face of Iron Man and the Hulk. Fortunately, God desires that we grow up and leave our movie stars and comic book heroes behind so that we may be molded by Him into the image of the only true hero, Jesus Christ.

THE DANGER OF PRIDE

Accountability relationships are often undervalued in the body of Christ because we have been deceived by pride, the ancient weapon of our archenemy, Satan. We have no desire to be vulnerable because pride has blinded us to our need for vulnerability. This perceived lack of need for accountability is precisely why we must be accountable to others.

At its most basic level, pride deceives and blinds us to the truth. Pride fools you into thinking you are not foolish. It leads you to think too highly of yourself. It may infect you in a moment and remain for a lifetime.

It was pride which led Satan to believe he should be enthroned above God in Heaven, and it is pride which leads us to enter our days in any posture other than absolute dependence upon God for our every need.

Pride tricks you into believing you are right, no matter how wrong you are. When pride has taken hold in an area of your life, it will blind you to its existence, and render you virtually incapable of detecting it in yourself. It solidifies lies, alienates you from abiding in the presence of God, and drives you away from those who would correct you.

Pride finds its seedbed in the very core of our being. As beings created in the image of God, our consciences were placed within us to demand that we do what is right. However, Romans 1 and 2 reveal that the human conscience may become corrupted. In the end, a seared conscience will justify all manner of evil.

This self-justification is evidenced in Proverbs 21:2, where we read "every way of a man is right in his own eyes" (KJV). This passage is a telling diagnosis of the human condition. Hitler slaughtered millions of Jews because he believed it was right to institute the Third Reich by any means necessary. Suicide bombers have detonated themselves because they believed it was right to destroy the enemies of their god. Although these are extreme examples, we need to be aware that the human heart will justify itself regardless of its level of depravity.

To wisely counter the power of pride, the blindness it creates, and our destructive tendency to justify even our sinful behaviors, someone you trust *must* have access to your life. A trusted friend should be given the freedom to shine the light of truth on the dark areas of your life. Pardon the redundancy, but you need others to inform you of your blind spots because you are blind to them!

Satan wants to keep you in the dark. He is a master at employing deception and self-justification to corrupt the purity of your heart and misdirect the course of your life. He passionately works to stunt your growth in godliness and holiness. He loves to make fools of those who carry the name of Christ. An accountability partner will alert you when you have practically lost the ability to alert yourself. Seek God for an accountability partner. Two heads are better than one.

COMMITMENT TO COMMUNITY

I Peter 4:12 states, "Each of you should use whatever gift you have received to serve others, as faithful stewards of God's grace in its various forms." The third practical necessity is to commit and entrust yourself to a community of believers.

The origin of community is found in the person of God, who is at once Father, Son, and Holy Spirit. As far as can be discerned from the whole of scripture, we are led to believe God has forever existed in a loving relationship within the three persons of the Godhead. The Father has always loved the Son, and the Son the Spirit. Furthermore, Christ taught a small community of disciples who were tasked with the charge to take His message to the entire community of mankind.

The entire universe springs from community, exists by the will of community, and finds its ultimate fulfillment in community. In short, we were made by community and for community. We minister to one another, live life together, serve together, worship together, and reach the world together in community. And ultimately, we will spend eternity together in community in Heaven.

In our judicial system, attorneys are tasked with providing persuasive evidence to the court, and the jury is tasked with the duty of considering all evidence submitted and handing down a verdict. In the case regarding your role within the community of Christ, the evidence has been submitted and the verdict has been delivered.

God knew you before you were born (Jeremiah 1:5), and chose you before the foundation of the world to be adopted as His child (Ephesians 1:5). God chose the time period and place where you were to be born (Acts 17:26), crafted you in your mother's womb (Psalm 139:13), and numbered the very hairs on your head (Luke 12:7).

God placed you within the body of Christ (I Corinthians 12:27), gave you spiritual gifts (I Corinthians 12:7), and commands that you use your gifts to serve others (I Corinthians 12:7). Therefore, we are not to give up meeting together (Hebrews 11:25).

The local church, as the most immediate example of the larger body of Christ, is the arena in which Christians come together to love Christ, worship Christ, minister Christ, and be ministered to by Christ. We should not take our commitment to it lightly. Our level of commitment to our local church is a mirror of our commitment to Christ.

The significance of your role in the body of Christ extends beyond the local church to the farthest corners of the earth. Jesus calls you "the salt of the earth" and "the light of the world" (Matthew 5:13-14). God has actually chosen you to work with Him in bringing the good news to all people groups, and has tasked you with the duty to make disciples of all nations (Matthew 28:19-20).

The church, both local and international, is the living, breathing presence of Christ on this earth. When we serve the church by expressing our spiritual gifts, God ministers by His Spirit in our midst (I Corinthians 12:6). When we give to the church, we give to Christ, and when we fail to give to the church we fail to give to Christ (Matthew 25:40).

As mature believers we should view the work of God inside us and inside our local church as part of the greater movement of the Kingdom of God throughout human history. Remember, we are a "a chosen people, a royal priesthood, a holy nation, God's special possession" (I Peter 2:9). Christ did not design us to be loners. We are part of the body of Christ, heirs of God and co-workers with all the saints present, past, and future. We have been called and set apart by God to serve as priests before Him.

Just down the street in your local church there are those who are in need of the healing touch of your spiritual gifts. Get down there and allow Christ to use you. Now is the time for you to rise up and take your position as a servant leader in His kingdom. He has raised you for such a time as this.

Your potential as a child of God is inextricably linked to your commitment to your local church. Your church may go door-to-door in your neighborhood, conduct a backyard bible club, or sponsor a child or missionary. We do this together.

You will not properly move down the tracks of the Kingdom of God unless you are attached to the locomotive of your local church. Every church member on earth needs the ministry of Christ through other believers, and every culture on earth needs the saving grace of Jesus Christ. In Christ, you have what your church and your culture needs and you are called to go and take Him to them.

I am reminded of Shakespeare's verse in *As You Like It* which reads "all the world's a stage, and all the men and women merely players. They have their exits and their entrances; and one man in his time plays many parts." Play your part in your local church wholeheartedly. Play it well.

I encourage you to press forward in your practice of these three practical steps. Realize you are a child of the truth. Christ desires that you have a pure heart and delights to see truth in your inmost being (Psalms 51:6). Being authentic syncs your life with the reality and truth of Christ. It sets you free from Satan's plot to enslave you in the service of your self-image.

Do you want to be the dreaded hypocrite? If not, then allow the cleansing fire of God to burn away all that is fake, pretend, or put-on. Allow Christ to make you comfortable with your weakness, and He will entrust you with His great strength. You don't have to be beautiful, athletic, intelligent, or cool. You do have to be yourself. When we live to please others we cease to please Christ (Galatians 1:10). Authenticity will free you from the shackles of being a people-pleaser and set you free to be who God wants you to be. Don't mistake your audience. Please Christ, and let everyone else think what they may.

As for accountability, your walk with God with take off like a rocket if you simply humble yourself and ask fellow believers for help. The infant begs for milk. The poor man begs for bread. The lover of God begs for accountability. You must hedge yourself in with the help of trusted believers. Don't miss out on the golden opportunity to invite others to assist you in your pursuit of making your blind spots your bulls-eye.

Kiss your isolation goodbye. Wisdom and experience teach that we are inconsistent, easily derailed, and in need of correction. Accept the instruction of wisdom. Ask God to show you ways in which your pride is hindering your walk with Him, and if you want it bad enough, then be brave and ask others to confront your pride as well. Position your life for integrity. Go for it, even if you are the only member of your church in an accountability relationship.

Regarding your commitment to your church, why should you choose to be a bench warmer when you can be a starter? If you are failing to engage your gifts in your local church, and are failing to take part as your church seeks to make disciples of all nations, then you are warming your team's bench. The battle is being fought at this very moment by the power of Christ within the community of believers called the church. The Kingdom of God is ever moving forward. Why should you be left behind?

If you are making excuses how you have no time left for your local church, and avoiding the commitment to become actively involved in ministering to your fellow believers and reaching a lost world, then STOP. Pray for God to show you how to engage your gifts in the ministry of your church, then obey when He shows you where to take part.

Recognize your participation in the move of God through a local church is not a one-act play, or a passing fad, but a lifelong commitment. See your work in your local church as a foundational part of your investment in eternity. Pray for wisdom to discern those who are on the perimeter or fringe of engaging in your local church. Christ loves His lost sheep. Let Him use you to pull them in.

Godliness requires discipline. If you want to press forward towards eternity with all your might, then practice these practical necessities. If you are hungry for spiritual growth, eat of their fruit. If they present a challenge, then ask God to give you a dogged determination to implement them. Now is your chance. Now is your time to position yourself to become a mature child of the Most High.

CHAPTER 7
LOVING GOD WITH ALL YOUR MIND:
THE CALL TO ENGAGE YOUR MIND

As children we are taught the greatest commandment is to "love the Lord your God with all your heart and with all your soul and with all your strength *and with all your mind*" (Luke 10:27, emphasis mine). Yet, in spite of how frequently we quote this verse, it appears we are still a little foggy about loving God with our mind. That last little four-letter word of the greatest commandment is often overlooked, ignored, and misunderstood. How on earth do we love God with all our mind?

Try for a moment to remember back to your grade school days and the excitement you had on the last day of school before summer vacation. Remember the anticipation of being free from the classroom for the entire summer?

The school would be abuzz with a fevered excitement. The teachers were giddy. Kids were on the verge of spontaneous combustion. Even the janitors wore a smile. We stood at the edge of the prison doors and longed to be set free from the compulsion to study and learn.

Some kids enjoyed this feeling so much they decided to forego their educational pursuits in order to pursue the elusive unending summer vacation. Sadly, it appears many believers adopt a similar drop-out mentality, and seek an extended vacation from fully engaging their minds in their relationship with Christ.

They fail to remember a disciple is a student, and allow their distaste for mental exertion to translate into mental and intellectual laziness and neglect. In short, they fail to love God with all their mind.

"Let the one who boasts boast about this: that they have the understanding to know me" (Jeremiah 9:24). As a student of Christ, you are called to take part in the mentally rigorous pursuit of knowing and understanding God. You cannot divorce your mind from your faith.

God created our minds to consider His words, to study His ways, and to apply our intellect to truth. We are of those who sit as Mary did at the feet of Christ. We long to hear from our Master and learn His ways. We grow in our love of our Father as we spend time listening, learning, and then applying and sharing the truths He has taught us.

When you signed your name on the dotted line with Christ He expected you to engage your mind with Him throughout the remainder of your time on earth. It doesn't matter what you scored on your I.Q. test, or whether you enjoy reading or studying, God gave you the raw materials He desired for you to have, and you can and must engage with the mind He has given you.

You may argue that you are no great thinker, no natural lover of learning, or that you see no place for employing your mind in your faith. However, the command remains: "Do your best to present yourself to God as one approved, a worker . . . who correctly handles the word of truth" (2 Timothy 2:15). There is no opt-out provision allowing you to place your mind on ice and proceed only with your heart, soul, and strength. Your mind belongs to Christ, and He intends for you to use it.

We must understand and teach others that loving God with our mind is a central part of our relationship with God. As we discussed earlier, if we love God we will obey His commands, and He commands us to love Him with our mind. The opposite is also true: if we fail to love God with our minds, then we are failing to love God in the way He desires and are stopping short of complete obedience.

Our sinful nature naturally looks to travel the path of least resistance. We are incredibly comfortable with our creature comforts, both physical and mental, and often resist any threat to them. Nevertheless, if you are serious about loving God you will be forced to take the road less traveled. You will be forced to engage all of your abilities, including your mind, to push forward into deeper levels of knowledge, intimacy, and obedience. Come on, summer vacation is over and class is back in session. To aid you in your pursuit of loving God with all of your mind, I encourage you to take two practical steps.

SETTING YOUR MIND ON THINGS ABOVE

"Set your minds on things above, not on earthly things" (Colossians 3:2). In order to love God with all your mind, you must first choose to set your mind on the things of God. The habit of setting our minds on *something* is already in place, the challenge is to think on *things above*. We are to start and end our days thinking about Him and praying to Him, listening to Him and learning from Him. When we drift away we are to come back to him again and again.

The King James Version translates this verse "Set your affection on things above, not on the things that are on the earth." The natural drift of a lover is to the object of his love. So it is with God. If we love Him, we will think about Him.

As we train our minds to think about God, He becomes the object of our affection and our attention, and our minds are transformed by Him. In Romans 12:2 Paul wrote, "Do not conform to the pattern of this world, but be transformed by the renewing of your mind." God has decreed you are to be made new, and this renewal takes place by His transformation of your mind as you dwell on things above.

Rome wasn't built in a day. The command to engage your mind and refocus your thoughts on the invisible is another lifelong challenge. Setting your mind on things above is a habit which will require practice, repetition, and growth, but continue to push forward.

As you begin to grow in the mastery of your thought life, you will become increasingly more aware of opportunities to invest in eternity. Over time, you will begin to mature in your ability to see and live life from an eternal perspective.

In turn, the soil of your mind will become a rich field for the thoughts of Christ to spring forth from within you (I Corinthians 2:16). The thoughts of Christ within your mind will then move you to think and do things your earthly mind would never conceive. This is the cycle by which a sinful mind overcomes its earthbound, self-centered patterns of thinking, and is transformed into the instrument of God it was originally designed to be.

Begin setting your mind on things above by centering your life around prayer and the Word of God. God has commanded that we love Him with all of our mind, and only God can give us the strength to accomplish so great a challenge.

Plead with God to hold you close to His throne. Speak with Him about everything. Ask Him to make your mind new, to realign your focus on Him, and to give you the tools and encouragement you need to see this discipline grow into maturity. Pray that your focus on preparing to meet Christ will be renewed over and over throughout your life. Ask expecting His answer, and continue to ask until He brings it to pass.

As you pray, saturate your thoughts with the Word of God. When you meditate on the Word you bring the thoughts and things of God to bear upon your mind. Although it is great to have a daily reading time, to better grasp the richness of God's Word you must also allow the Word to remain with you throughout the day.

Take a verse from your daily reading and meditate on it throughout the day. Talk about it with classmates, co-workers, or friends. Write the verse on a note card and place it in a prominent place. Pray the verse before God and ask for His wisdom to help you see how it should be applied in your life. In short, place a premium on the Word of God.

I am not suggesting you view this discipline as a new self-help regime, but as a vital part of your walk with Christ throughout the remainder of your time on earth. If you commit to pray for God's strength to set your mind on things above, and take concrete steps to practice the awareness of His presence and fill your mind with His Word, you will be squarely on the path to loving God with all of your mind.

TAKING YOUR THOUGHTS CAPTIVE

Each moment of each day will test your commitment to set your mind on things above. Impure thoughts will invade your mind, while worries, fears, and regrets will attempt to distract your focus. You will be forced to wage war against the thoughts that challenge the rule of Christ in your mind.

Paul states in 2 Corinthians 10:3-5 "Though we live in the world, we do not wage war as the world does. The weapons we fight with are not the weapons of the world. On the contrary, they have divine power to demolish strongholds. We demolish arguments and every pretension that sets itself up against the knowledge of God, and we take captive every thought to make it obedient to Christ."

Locked inside this passage is a precious and powerful discipline which will allow you to make great strides in your thought life. The discipline is commonly called *taking your thoughts captive*.

Paul states in unequivocal terms we are in the midst of a war. However, the war in which we are engaged is not fought with the weapons of this world (v.4). Our weapons as Christians are not to be found stockpiled in an arsenal or sitting at the tip of a missile in an underground silo. Our weapons are invisible, supernatural, of God.

As a good soldier needs to know how to skillfully use his earthly weapons, we need to understand how to skillfully use our divine weapons. One such weapon is the power to take our thoughts captive.

I remember being introduced to this tactic of spiritual warfare by my high school youth minister. Although I was amazed to learn God had given me the power to take dominion over my thoughts, I had no way of knowing how this discipline would save me from innumerable worries, fears, and anxieties over the course of my life.

As children of truth, we are given power to isolate and

seize untrue thoughts. Untrue thoughts destroy our peace, steal our joy, and enslave us to lies, thus hindering our ability to love God with all of our mind. These thoughts place us in the suffocating grip of worry, fear, doubt, lust, and other slavish thoughts, and they continually and desperately war against the lordship of Christ. Put simply, they *must* be overtaken, seized, and removed from a position of influence in our minds.

The process of taking your thoughts captive begins the moment you decide to establish truth as the foundation of your life. You must love, honor, and subject every area of your life to truth. Christ Himself stated "I am . . . the truth" (John 14:6).

To the degree we submit every thought to the truth, we submit to Christ, and to the degree we fail to submit every thought to truth, we fail to submit to Christ. You cannot exempt any thought of your mind from obedience to Christ. A thought exempted from the truth of Christ is ground gained by the enemy.

By stating we are to make our thoughts "obedient to Christ" (v.5), Paul assumes that we have an intimate knowledge of what Christ commands. Our knowledge of the truth informs us which thoughts are to be kept and which are to be taken captive. However, a lack of knowledge of the Word of God impedes our ability to grasp which thoughts are to be honored and which are to be rejected.

Attempting to filter impure and corrupt thoughts without a solid grasp of what is pure and true would be similar to attempting to referee a sporting event without having knowledge of the rules. This is where the importance of being a student comes into clear focus.

We cannot expect to master the enemies of our minds if we are unwilling to take the time to equip our minds for battle. We must make ourselves students of the word of God so that we are able to discern truth from error. We must learn in the classroom of everyday experience and in the solitude of quiet study, in the interactions of the workplace and by interaction with Christ in the prayer closet.

Only when we are capable of sorting and distinguishing our thoughts in the light of God's Word will we be able to bind the error so that the truth may prevail. As a student of Christ, it should be your desire to become like one of the mature students of the Word of God "who through constant use have trained themselves to distinguish good from evil" (Hebrews 5:14).

EVERYDAY EXAMPLES

In principle you may agree that taking your thoughts captive is a necessity, but still be unclear as to how to practice the discipline in your everyday life, so let's take a look at how this often works.

Let's assume you have chosen to set your mind on things above, and Christ is becoming the object of your deepest affection and attention. You are laboring daily to pray, think about Him, and meditate on His Word. Furthermore, you have enshrined truth as the litmus test by which every thought must be judged, and as the siphon through which every thought must pass.

The process of taking your thoughts captive begins the moment you recognize you are thinking about something which is causing you to move your mind off course from Christ. You may notice a particular thought is causing you mental or emotional anguish, or leading you to think other harmful, sinful thoughts. Sometimes you may need to analyze your chain of thoughts in reverse, going backward through your thoughts, until you are able to pinpoint the thought which is the source of your trouble.

The thought to be bound can be one of doubt, fear, worry, lust, anger, jealousy, or any of a host of impure and destructive thoughts. Whatever the thought, it is one which has set itself up in your mind as "against the knowledge of God" (I Corinthians 3:5). In other words, at its core the thought strikes against your knowledge of who God is and the truth He has revealed to us.

Once a thought is recognized as an enemy of truth, it is

helpful to isolate and state the thought. This is similar to what happens when a bailiff brings an inmate into open court to be formally charged. Whether you choose to do this silently or verbally, it involves stating what the thought is speaking into your mind. This may sound hocus pocus and smack of casting away an evil spell, but this isolation must take place in some form if you are to overcome and take the thought captive.

Don't be surprised if you find that you often fail to recognize you are being plagued by an evil thought until you have labored for a season under its harmful influence. Also, it is often difficult and time consuming to mentally distinguish between emotions and the thoughts which create them. In either case, don't lose heart; you will get better at this. The most deadly Green Beret was once just another raw recruit at boot camp.

Once you have recognized and named the thought, you must then take the thought captive (v.5). Again, this is where your work as a student in immersing your mind in truth comes to fruition. You are to confine and put the thought on trial, with Truth being the presiding judge. The thought must be judged in light of what is true, and if the thought is not in line with what scripture says is true, the thought must be condemned.

At times the thought will be easily recognized as untrue, and on other occasions it will be necessary for you to seek godly counsel regarding the thought. At this point, your work is almost complete.

After you have taken the thought captive, the final step is to make the thought obedient to Christ (v.5). This step is similar to the sentencing phase of a criminal trial, where a judge recites the law, condemns the convict of breaking it, and orders the convict to prison.

We make evil thoughts obedient to Christ by forcing them to submit to the truth and then ordering them to leave our minds. This can be done quietly or loudly, in any bodily posture you are led to assume. It doesn't matter what you look like. What matters is whether you are taking authority over the evil thought in the name of Jesus Christ, and replacing the lie with truth.

For example, a man may recognize he is allowing himself to lust after a woman. He must first recognize and name the thought as lust. He then takes the lustful thought captive and subjects the lust to the truth of God's Word. This can be done by recalling or stating that Jesus commanded us not to commit adultery in our hearts, and that the thought has no rightful place in his mind.

Finally, he makes the lustful thought obedient to Christ by speaking the truth over the thought and ordering it to leave his thoughts. By overtaking the thought with truth, and ordering the thought to leave, the thought of lust is sentenced to death and purged from the man's mind. When, or if the thought returns, the process is repeated until victory is won.

Another example would be a woman who recognizes she is struggling with self-esteem. She must first recognize which thoughts are leading her to feel this way, and name them. There may be a whole host of thoughts layered within her heart. If so, she needs to take a pen and pencil and begin to copy them.

Once she has recognized and named the thoughts, she judges the thoughts in the court of truth and speaks truth over the thoughts. For instance, she may recall that God loves her deeply and has deemed her to be the object of his affection. Furthermore, because she is worthy of the love of God through Christ, she is of great importance in the plan of God. After speaking truth over the lie, she orders the wicked thought from her mind and fills the void with the truth of her great value before God.

I would love to promise that neither the man nor the woman in the examples above will ever have to battle again with thoughts of lust or low self-esteem, but unfortunately this is not always the case. Some thoughts won't die so easily. Sometimes our victory is temporary. In some cases, we have to battle in prayer with the same thoughts multiple times before we gain the upper hand in overcoming their evil influence.

Some thoughts are so engrained and habitual that it may take weeks, months, or even years of consistently taking them captive before they can at last be conquered. We must not succumb to discouragement when we find ourselves speaking the truth over the same lie over and over again. You can do this! The Devil has no rightful ownership over any of our thoughts (Ephesians 4:27).

It is a huge step forward to determine you will set your mind on things above, but an altogether different step to control the battlefield of your mind by taking your thoughts captive on a daily basis. You must set your mind on things above **and** wage war against the deceptive thoughts that seek to corrupt and divert your focus. By doing so, you will become adept at isolating and imprisoning thoughts that rise up in defiance of truth.

Your enemy is relentless, and you are to counter and overcome his relentlessness by your resolve to consistently apply the power of truth. By the power of Christ and your persistency you have the power to bind the thoughts that blur your focus on eternity. You serve a God who has conquered death, hell, and every sinful thought under the sun. His victory is your victory.

"If you falter in a time of trouble, how small is your strength" (Proverbs 24:10). As a basketball player I was often challenged to take a "gut-check." A gut-check involves asking yourself the uncomfortable question of whether you have the heart and desire to get the job done. It means laying aside any hint of pretending or hiding so that you can be real with yourself and the team.

At this point I would like you to take a gut-check. Are you committed to laying it all on the line to make certain that you fully obey God, even it means engaging your mind in ways you never have? Are you willing to accept the mantle of *Student*, and renew your commitment to read, study, memorize, and meditate upon the Word of God? Your desire will play a huge part in this process. You must want it.

As I stated earlier, this fight is not for the timid, but for the bold. Your mind is precious to Christ. You cannot afford to squander its value to the Kingdom by fixing your mind on the things of earth. We must engage our minds if we are to love the Lord with all our mind.

Apply yourself with the intellect God has given you. Lift your mind up to the high and exalted, and God will open your eyes to the humble and lowly. If you sow thoughts that please Him, and pull the weeds from the garden of your mind, then you will reap a mindset which prompts you to invest in eternity.

CHAPTER 8
FINISHING STRONG:
THE CALL TO COMPLETION

You are in the race of a lifetime. "Run in such a way as to get the prize" (I Corinthians 9:24). As a student-athlete at Liberty University in Lynchburg, Virginia, my basketball coaches would often urge me to "Finish strong." At times it felt as if those two words haunted my very existence. Just before the completion of our workouts, whether running hills or wind sprints, lifting weights or doing defensive drills, the call was often the same: "Finish strong!" Although as a young man it was a bitter pill to swallow, as a middle-aged man the advice has proven itself wise.

The challenge to invest your time in eternity is a challenge which will require perseverance. The moment you chose to follow Christ, a bulls-eye was affixed upon you by Satan, "the accuser of our brothers" (Revelation 12:10). You are now a mortal enemy of the greatest evil power in the universe. Your enemy, Satan, "prowls around like a roaring lion looking for someone to devour" (I Peter 5:8).

Jesus stated Satan "was a murderer from the beginning" (John 8:44). His work is to steal, kill, and destroy, and he has proven himself adept at his work for thousands of years.

When Satan sees Christ, he sees the One who will ultimately hurl him into the lake of fire for all of eternity (Revelation 20:10), and you are a walking manifestation of Christ. The bright light of Christ shines from within you. Therefore, when Satan sees you, he sees Christ within you, and recognizes you as one who has authority and power in Christ to disrupt his work of destruction on the earth.

You remind Satan of his final destiny. What is more, he knows full well that by the gospel you preach he is exposed, conquered, and souls are set free from his vicious tyranny. Your very words signal his defeat and death.

Beware of his desire to knock you out of the race. "No one who puts his hand to the plow and looks back is fit for service in the kingdom of God" (Luke 9:62). Because Satan is fully aware of the lethal power of Christ within you, He will seek in every conceivable way to neutralize the great threat presented by your complete submission to Christ.

If you lose your focus and take your hands off the plow, you will begin the natural drift into the ever present danger of complacency and powerlessness. Our duty is urgent and our enemy is cunning, so we must keep our hands on the plow until we pierce the veil and see His face. To that end, let's focus on our call to completion.

THE INEVITABILITY OF TRIALS

Job stated "Man that is born of woman is of few days and full of trouble." (Job 14:1, KJV). We need to discard the myth that the Christian life is a bed of roses. The high road to completion in Christ often passes through the low valleys of trials. Life on earth is often marked by persecution, the consequences of sin, and even the loving discipline of our Heavenly Father.

Jesus flatly denied the possibility of a primrose path in His teachings, by His life, and through His death. In John 15:20 Christ stated "A servant is not greater than his master. If they persecuted me, they will persecute you also." If we desire to follow the path of our Master with a whole heart, we will face persecution.

Paul echoed the same when he stated, "In fact, everyone who wants to live a godly life in Christ Jesus will be persecuted" (2 Timothy 3:12). These statements are not suggestions of a possibility or probability, but are promises. There is no wiggle room left for the Christian seeking to avoid the hard reality of our calling.

We don't have to dig deeply in our library to see these promises fulfilled in the lives of Christ and Paul, and then in the lives of the early disciples. Christian tradition records every single disciple of Christ died the death of a martyr, except John, who was exiled for his faith on Patmos after undergoing severe persecution.

Beginning with the early church, and continuing until the present day, there has been a long train of persecution against the followers of Christ. It is little wonder, for Satan is "filled with fury, knowing that his time is short." (Revelation 12:12).

In addition to the persecution we face from the forces of Satan and the deceived patrons of his lies, we are also forced to deal with the common consequences of sin. Although we are not of this world, we are certainly in it. We reap what we sow, and often reap what others have sown. We worry, we fear, and we suffer from disease. We hurt others, others hurt us, and we hurt ourselves. Take a trip through your local homeless shelter, prison, or nursing home, and this reality will be deeply impressed upon your soul.

Another source of trials is the discipline of our loving Father. "My son, do not despise the Lord's discipline, and do not resent his rebuke, because the Lord disciplines those he loves, as a father the son he delights in." (Proverbs 3:11-12).

The perfect love of our God will not allow us to remain in unrepentant sin, or allow us to permanently stagnate in our growth. His great love, along with his mercy toward us, compels Him to move us forward in the development of our Christ-like character. And glory to God this is so! Otherwise, we would tend to become like the ancient Israelites about whom the prophet Amos stated "Woe to them that are at ease in Zion" (Amos 6:1, KJV).

Please don't take me for a kill-joy. Joy is our inheritance from Christ. "I have told you this so that my joy may be in you and that your joy may be complete" (John 15:11). I am not suggesting you allow the reality of trials to destroy your joy, nor do I suggest you spend your life constantly peeking around the corner for the next problem. Of all people on earth, we should be the ones sucking the most marrow from our existence and looking most expectantly to the great thing God is about to do next.

However, do not consider the easy yoke and light burden of Christ as an exemption from trials. In the divine plan of God, trials are a necessary part. Therefore, in order to live a life of joy during the rough times, we need to understand how God uses trials to move us forward in our race to eternity.

THE PURPOSE OF TRIALS

Rather than cower in the corner during times of trouble, we must see our trials for what they are and exploit their great potential in our lives. In James 1:2-4 the Apostle urges us to "Consider it pure joy, my brothers and sisters, whenever you face trials of many kinds, because you know that the testing of your faith produces perseverance. Let perseverance finish its work so that you may be mature and complete, not lacking anything."

This passage is key to understanding the purpose of trials. James urges us to do the unthinkable - to consider it *pure joy* to undergo trials. Wow. This is a bewildering proposition, especially when we consider the effort and resources we expend avoiding anything and everything which might in *some way* be uncomfortable.

Before you convince yourself that James had a temporary lapse of reason, let's push deeper into the teaching. Why would James say we should consider it pure joy to undergo trials? "Because *you know that the testing of your faith develops perseverance.*" (v.3, emphasis mine) Trials are the crucible within which God forms the much needed character quality of perseverance.

Why does God desire to develop our perseverance? If we fail to persevere, we fail to keep pace with the Spirit, and fail to shine the light of Christ with the pure power He wishes to portray in and through us. Rather than being conquerors, we fall into the ranks of the conquered. However, once trials are viewed as a tool God uses to develop our perseverance, we can seize the wonderful opportunities they provide to strengthen our staying power.

In spite of the great importance of perseverance, James goes on to teach that perseverance is not the ultimate goal of trials. God develops our perseverance so that we "may be mature and complete, not lacking anything" (v.4). Trials develop perseverance, and perseverance brings us to completion in Christ. Let's not miss the forest for the trees. We don't celebrate trials for their pain. The purpose of facing trials with joy, and in developing perseverance, is our completion in Christ.

We are a work in progress. We are here for a very short time, and God has a big work to do in and through us. His desire is that we lack nothing (v.4). He is intent on preparing his bride for her groom, Jesus Christ. He will use circumstances we consider detestable and uncomfortable to make us ready for our eternal marriage to Christ. The old man must die, and the sharp sword of trials is quite the executioner.

VICTORY IN TRIALS

Trials represent routine pruning in the greenhouse of God. They are not fun, and most of us will never be the first in line to volunteer for a trial. Yet we have been given the divine ability to see trials for what they are: divinely ordained character builders. Because we are more than conquerors in Christ, we have the power to make the most of every opportunity they provide.

There is no magic recipe for overcoming trials. We just continue to do the basics, putting one foot in front of the other until the storm passes. We remain authentic, accountable, and committed to a community of believers. We abide in Christ, and continue working passionately for him in spite of the obstacles which would lure us into self-loathing, isolation, or complacency. We keep our focus on the things of God, and take captive every thought that might lead us to pity ourselves or become angry with God.

Fortunately most trials prove to be temporary. We usually arrive alive and well at the end of our trials. Christ is with us in the midst of our troubles, and ever moving us forward, sustaining and comforting us as we keep in step with His Spirit. We may emerge with a bruised ego, a broken bone, or a big scar, but we come out standing no matter the death the trial has inflicted upon our old self.

I encourage you to remain faithful if you are in the midst of a trial. You will make it through if you remain firm in Christ. Many have trod this path before you and have proven that trials can and must be endured. As you struggle through your deepest and darkest times, the chorus of Heaven is singing over you, and the Author of your salvation is writing a new and beautiful chapter in your book. He is bringing forth a diamond from the coal, to His praise. Persevere that you may become complete. Persevere so that you can look back with a smile and glorify your Faithful Father.

FINISHING STRONG

A dear friend once rhetorically asked how much money I would have invested in Apple stock in the 1980's had I known what the future would hold for the company. The obvious answer was EVERYTHING I reasonably could invest.

Although we're not dealing with stock here, we do have a sure investment on our hands. Our lives will be rewound before the judge of the whole earth and we will see how we invested. God has given us the wisdom to see the certainty of our predicament, and commanded us to store up treasures for ourselves in Heaven. Let's invest while we can! We have no time to waste, and no reason to hold anything back. We must seize every opportunity to buy into eternity. We must finish strong!

Hopefully, this book has helped you recognize the incredible importance of your time on earth and the eternal ramifications of the lifestyle you choose to live. If so, I will have succeeded in making a Divine Investment. Now, by the grace of God, I encourage you to spend the remainder of your days preparing to stand before Christ unashamed, and encouraging others to do the same. May you make your life a Divine Investment, and may we shake hands with a smile on the other side of the veil.

THE DIVINE INVESTMENT
SMALL GROUP STUDY GUIDE

The following small group study guide has been created to provide simple questions group leaders may use to facilitate discussion. The study guide can be used with every age group from teenagers through senior citizens. The questions build upon one another and are designed to methodically lead a group through the flow of each chapter. May your group be blessed as you prayerfully lead them in the study of truth, and remember: "If any man speak, let him speak as the oracles of God" (I Peter 4:11).

CHAPTER 1
DEFINING THE DIVINE INVESTMENT

1. How often do you spend time thinking about *forever*? Why or why not?

2. Does the idea of forever scare or comfort you? Why?

3. Do you think it is important to consider forever? Why?

4. Regarding our time on earth, notice Psalms 103:15-16: "As for man his days are as grass: as a flower of the field so he flourisheth. For the wind passeth over it and it is gone; and the place thereof shall know it no more" (KJV).

5. Picture a dandelion and how easily its florets are blown into the wind: have you ever considered your life on earth to be as tender and brief as the dandelion?

6. Regarding our time in eternity, read I Thessalonians 4:17 and Matthew 25:41: notice that in contrast to our time on earth, both destinations named are eternal.

7. If one destination of our spirit is incredibly short (earth), and one is immeasurably long (eternity), what does this say about the amount of energy we should devote to each?

8. Are you aware that every word you speak (Matthew 12:36) and every work you do (I Corinthians 3:13-15) will be brought before Christ in judgment?

9. Group Leaders, be careful at this point to establish that faith in Christ, and not good works, is how we inherit eternal life (Ephesians 2:8-10), and the judgment we are speaking of is a judgment of the quality of our work as children of God.

10. If you believe that you will stand before Christ for your works on earth, how important is it to prepare for that day? Why?

11. At this point, you should lead the discussion to its logical conclusion: How do we prepare? We now introduce the concept of *The Divine Investment*.

12. What does divine mean? What are some examples?

13. What is an investment? What do people invest in?

14. What is *The Divine Investment?* It is an investment of your life in eternity, a life lived in preparation of meeting Christ.
15. Why does it make sense to make your life count for *forever?*

CHAPTER 2
GO BIG OR GO HOME:
THE CALL TO REPENTANCE

1. How can the phrase "go big or go home" relate to your walk with Christ?

2. Are you going big for God at this time in your life? If so, how? If not, why not?

3. Read Luke 12:16-20.

4. In what ways does your life resemble the fool in this passage?

5. If someone in your family or inner circle of friends was asked to describe your life, would he or she describe your life as one set on fire by God and burning passionately with a desire to know Him? Or would they say you are all about yourself and your goals, and making yourself happy? Or somewhere in-between? Are you content with what their response would be?

6. Do you aspire for your life to exhibit a heroic Christian faith like the Apostle Paul, Mother Teresa, or Jim Elliott?

7. At this point shift the discussion to repentance.

8. What is repentance?

9. How do we repent?

10. When do we repent?

11. Do you feel that you need to repent and make it you life goal to push deeper into intimacy with Christ? To focus the remainder of your life on preparing for eternity? To seek to accomplish God's purposes for your life?

12. Challenge them to "go big."

13. Read 2 Timothy 2:20-21, and discuss.

14. Do you believe that God really wants to use you to do things of eternal importance and value?

15. Think for a moment on something you have really been wanting lately, something that is at the top of your list in life?

How strong is this desire, 1-10? Now, compare that desire to your desire to be used by God: which occupies more of your thoughts or energy?

16. Encourage the students to spend time in prayer and repentance, asking God for a renewed sense of urgency and urgency.

17. Encourage students to realize steps must be taken, and to spend the next week trying to see their lives and their interactions with others as being of cosmic importance.

CHAPTER 3
MAKING DIFFICULT DECISIONS:
THE CALL TO ABANDONMENT

1. How often do you consider that Christ calls you to give up everything to Him?
2. On a day-to-day basis how are you giving up everything for Christ?
3. How are repentance and abandonment tied together in our walk with Christ?
4. Do you think repentance is real if not followed by abandonment of what you have repented of? Why or why not?
5. Why would God ask you to give up something?
6. How is abandoning something an act of faith?
7. What is your "will"?
8. How does your "will" work in your day-to-day life?
9. Why does God need your will?
10. How did Christ abandon His will? How should you abandon your will?
11. What does it mean that God is at work within you "to will and to act according to his good purpose?"
12. How often do you wake up and say "Jesus, you can have my time today – and especially my free time – to do whatever you want with me?"
13. Do you act as if your time is truly yours and not a gift from God to be used by Him?
14. Do you really believe that if you give your time to God He will use it for His glory? What is stopping you? Abandon it.
15. Do you look at your possessions as yours or as God's? Why?
16. What are ways God can use what you have for His kingdom and glory?

17. How can you begin living as if what you have belongs to God?

18. How does your understanding of possessions help you understand why being selfish is so wrong and ugly?

19. What are some examples you have seen of others who give what they have to the kingdom in small or large ways?

20. Final Point: The time for holding on has come and gone. Build on your repentance by abandoning whatever stands in the way of your progress.

CHAPTER 4
THE POWER OF YES:
THE CALL TO OBEDIENCE

1. Why do we not like being told what to do?

2. How does it make you feel when you read that Jesus said "If you love me, you will obey my commands?"

3. How does obedience show love?

4. Does it make sense to say "God, I love you," and **not** do what he says? Why or why not?

5. How does our obedience glorify God?

6. Why do you believe God wants glory?

7. Do you find it frustrating or comforting that you cannot understand everything about God? Why?

8. What would lead you to believe God commands you to do things because he loves you?

9. When you feel God is leading you to do something, how often do you stop and think that His love is leading Him to ask you?

10. When God asks you to do something do you see it more as a burden or as an opportunity to see a blessing come your way?

11. Discuss practical areas of obedience: forgiveness, bible study, prayer, etc.

12. Encourage the students to pin down specific areas in which God is leading them to obey.

CHAPTER 5
AWAITING ORDERS:
THE CALL TO ABIDE

1. What does it mean for an officer to stand "at attention?"
2. Why would God want you to stand at attention before Him?
3. How can you practically stand "at attention" before God?
4. Help the students understand that this is a discipline, a practice they will be engaging in until the day they die. Why is it necessary that we abide?
5. Why is it so hard to be still before God?
6. Give an example of what spiritual fruit looks like in everyday life.
7. Help the students understand that salvation is the **beginning** of good works and should be evidenced by good works.
8. Would a bystander see your life as one which produces good works? Do you see room for more in your life? Are you willing to pray and ask God for more opportunities. *Lead them in prayer.
9. Remind the students that their works will follow them into judgment. Read I Corinthians 3:13-15. Help them see the eternal nature of their acts on earth.

CHAPTER 6
PRACTICING THE PRACTICAL: THE CALL TO AUTHENTICITY, ACCOUNTABILITY, AND COMMUNITY

Authenticity – Being Real
1. Would your friends in church be surprised to see how you speak and act outside church?
2. When God looks at your heart, does He see a person who is honest and open with Him with their feelings or someone who hides them deep inside?
3. Why do we hide our feelings? Why is it important to be transparent before God?
4. Why is it important to sincere, honest, and real with others? What problems are caused when we are not honest with others?

Accountability
5. Have you ever thought about building an accountability relationship? What should you look for in an accountability partner (trustworthiness, honesty, etc.)?
6. Why do you think the bible teaches that two are better than one? How can a trusted friend help you in your walk with Jesus?
7. Do you believe that you can see things in your friends that even they cannot see about themselves? Is the same not true for you? BINGO. This is why you need an accountability partner.
8. Are you willing to ask God for an accountability partner?

Commitment to Community
9. Why is it important to be actively involved in a local church?
10. How often do you approach church thinking "How can I

be a blessing to someone in church today?"

11. How often do you consider your role as a worker in the local church as a significant part of your stewardship responsibilities before God?

12. Are you willing to make a commitment to always be in a local church exercising your spiritual gifts and seeking to blessing to others? If not, why?

CHAPTER 7
LOVING GOD WITH ALL YOUR MIND:
THE CALL TO ENGAGE YOUR MIND

<u>Loving God with Our Minds:</u>
1. Have you ever thought about what your mind has to do with your relationship with Christ?
2. What is a student of Christ? Why would Christ seek students?
3. Do you consider yourself a student of Christ? Why?

<u>Setting Our Minds on Things Above</u>
4. What do you spend most of your time thinking about?
5. About how much time do you spend each day consciously choosing to think about God, Christ, and eternity?
6. What daily disciplines do you have in place to train yourself to consistently think about God?
7. Are you willing to go home and schedule a quiet time from now until the end of the year that includes prayer and bible study?

<u>Taking Our Thoughts Captive</u>
8. What are some thoughts that haunt or hurt you?
9. Take time to walk the students through the process of isolating the lie, taking it captive; and then replacing the lie with truth.

CHAPTER 8
FINISHING STRONG:
THE CALL TO COMPLETION

Introduction
1. Why do we often fail to finish what we have started?
2. Do you think it will be easy or hard to finish the Christian life? Why?
3. How have you seen Satan attack others? How have you been attacked by Satan?

The Inevitability of Trials
4. Why would Jesus promise persecution?
5. How have you seen people persecuted? How have you been persecuted?
6. Have you had to suffer because of the sins of others?
7. Have you ever felt that God was disciplining you? How?
8. Why does God discipline his children?

The Purpose of Trials
9. Why is it important that a runner have perseverance ?
10. Why is it important for you to persevere in your Christian life?
11. How often do you think about God removing your impurities so that you can stand before Christ spotless and blameless? How do trials ready you for your wedding with Christ?

ABOUT THE AUTHOR

Will Roach is the current General Sessions and Juvenile Court Judge for Jefferson County, Tennessee. He studied theology and history at Oxford University, Vanderbilt Divinity School, and at The Southern Baptist Theological Seminary before graduating from Liberty University School of Law. Will is active in the international missions, prison, small group, and youth ministries of his local church, and is married with three children.

Made in the USA
Lexington, KY
12 April 2016